FINDING A HIDING PLACE

FINDING A HIDING PLACE:

Revealing God's Way

GENEVA SILVERNAIL

XULON PRESS

Xulon Press
555 Winderley Pl, Suite 225
Maitland, FL 32751
407.339.4217
www.xulonpress.com

© 2023 by Geneva Silvernail

All rights reserved solely by the author. The author guarantees all contents are original and do not infringe upon the legal rights of any other person or work. No part of this book may be reproduced in any form without the permission of the author.

Due to the changing nature of the Internet, if there are any web addresses, links, or URLs included in this manuscript, these may have been altered and may no longer be accessible. The views and opinions shared in this book belong solely to the author and do not necessarily reflect those of the publisher. The publisher therefore disclaims responsibility for the views or opinions expressed within the work.

Unless otherwise indicated, Scripture quotations taken from the Holy Bible, New International Version (NIV). Copyright © 1973, 1978, 1984, 2011 by Biblica, Inc.™. Used by permission. All rights reserved.

Paperback ISBN-13: 978-1-66288-374-3
Ebook ISBN-13: 978-1-66288-375-0

Table of Contents

Introduction 1
   Why Write a Memoir? 2
   An Obsession with Places to Hide 4

Living With an AUD Parent 7
   Learning to Hide 8
   Hiding in the Tent 11
   Mama Confronts Granny 14
   Daddy's Special Medicine 18
   The Butcher Knife 21
   Hiding under the Covers 25
   A Secret Club House 29
   Hiding in the Coal Shed 32
   Stuffing Sue in the Couch 36
   Holding On for Dear Life 39
   Running Out of Places to Hide 42
   A Picnic in the Cemetery 46
   Driving across the Loudon Bridge 49
   Learning When to Hide 52
   The Ugliest Doll in the World 55
   A Precious Hiding Place 59
   Coming Up the First Step 62
   The Good Old Boys 65
   Pulling in the Ropes 68
   Saying "No" to Daddy 73

The Impact of the Church 77
    Who Will Go and Tell? 78
    Our Church Can Be Your Home 81
    My Church Home Was Not Perfect 84
    They Know My Mama's Name 89

The Effects of Alcohol Use Disorder (AUD) 95
    My Siblings, the Survivors 96
    My Sister, the Protector 99
    My Brother, the Seeker .103
    Myself, the Runner 107

Remembering a Loving Childhood 119
    My Mother Loved Me .120
    My Daddy Loved Me .123
    My Real Father Loves Me 127
    If You Need Help 129

Introduction

Why Write a Memoir?

> *"For I know the plans I have for you,"* declares the Lord, *"plans to prosper you and not to harm you, plans to give you hope and a future"* (Jer. 29:11).

Grabbing the chain, Daddy kicked the chair out of the way while pulling down the door with its attached ladder. We sat huddled together, listening as threatening and angry sounds invaded our private, safe room. He had found our hiding place. He was coming! He was coming up the first step, coming up the second step, coming up the third step. We already knew the ending of the story.

I walked away from the platform with the campers begging to hear what happened next. I cheerfully waved goodbye and told them they would hear more at the next chapel service.

As the camp director gave directions for the next event, I waited patiently in the lobby for my own schedule. Suddenly, one of the campers ran into my arms, almost knocking me over. Weeping uncontrollably, she sobbed, "Am I the little girl you talked about in your story?" Hugging her, I explained that I was the little girl. I softly asked her if she needed help. "Yes, please help me," she cried, "I don't know where to hide."

I listened to her story. Her story was my story: a little girl seeking a hiding place to escape from an abusive father. I wrote down her name and information that the authorities might need. With her permission, I told the camp director about her problems. The next few days were filled with meetings with social workers, the camp nurse, her pastor, and camp counselor. At the end of the week, her camp counselor and pastor introduced the little girl to a person who would help her find a hiding place.

These few pages are not meant to be an autobiography but a collection of memories shared from my heart. I realize the memories may not be the same as my siblings due to our ages, our points of view, and even our personal biases, but they are my memories. I realize I may receive criticism from those who may not understand the need for me to share my memories. Except for a few shared experiences with my living siblings, I did not mention the names of people except for my ex-husband and siblings who are no longer living.

So why I am writing this memoir of my childhood experiences? Perhaps I write this to the person who is being physically, verbally, or emotionally abused by a person with AUD (alcohol use disorder) and want to assure them that help is available.

Perhaps I write this for the person struggling with AUD who, after contemplating the effects of the use of alcohol on loved ones, may be encouraged to seek help.

Perhaps I write this for the church leader who needs to be alert to the effects of AUD and help families spiritually and direct them to needed resources.

In reality, I am writing this memoir mostly as a personal journey in healing from the traumatic experiences of my own childhood with an AUD parent and its effect on my adult life and my siblings. I do not seek revenge against anyone who hurt me. I don't desire to judge them for their actions. I only desire to embrace the past and consider its effect on the person I am today.

My Prayer of Thanks

Dear Father,
Help me to be honest in my recall of feelings and events. In the recalling, help me to not seek revenge or desire to hurt anyone but to embrace each one as part of my journey with You. Thank You for helping me to remember and to keep forgiving. Amen.

An Obsession with Places to Hide

"You are my hiding place; you will protect me from trouble and surround me with songs of deliverance" (Ps. 32:7).

Glancing immediately around the first room in a new building, I imagine a hiding place behind a sofa or huge chair, in the choir loft, in a closet, or in a small room nearby. I wonder, "Is there an attic?" "Is there a basement?" "Is there a garage or shed?"

I am an adult, seventy-seven this year, but I feel like a skinny ten-year-old girl with her long, stringy hair pulled up high and wrapped tightly with a red rubber band. The thought of that ten-year-old looking for a hiding place goes swiftly through my mind while I continue to smile and talk to others around me. No one knows I am looking for a hiding place.

I once questioned my brothers and sisters, and they laughingly admitted to searching for a hiding place when they enter a new building. We briefly discuss where would be a good place to hide in the very room where we sat. Silence overcomes us, and momentarily, we are lost in our own memories and thoughts. No one asks why we look for a hiding place. But we know.

I'm not sure when this obsession with hiding places started, perhaps when I was a toddler. Even now while known by many as a well-organized and calm person, I know I need to find a hiding place in order to breathe easier and be at peace. I have discovered safe hiding places in each home I have lived in around the world. For example, in the Philippines, I found a hiding place in a closet with a moveable divider so I could get to the far end of the closet for storage. I could have hidden inside the attic in Papua New Guinea, where few houses have attics. No, I have never needed to use those hiding places, but I had peace knowing a hiding place was available. I have discovered a hiding place in my forever retirement home. No, I won't share with you where it is. If I tell, I won't feel safe.

My Prayer of Thanks

Dear Father,
I realize You are my true hiding place. I trust You to take care of me, but I still have that thought of looking for a hiding place when I enter a new building. I know You understand my background more than I do. Instead of erasing the reasons why I look for a hiding place, You have chosen to use my past fears and experiences for Your glory.

Thank You for allowing me to use my experiences in narrative preaching styles and in praying with children and adults who are victims of abuse. Help me to be faithful to the calling You have given me. Amen.

Living With an AUD Parent

Learning to Hide

"Be strong and courageous. Do not be afraid or terrified because of them, for the Lord your God goes with you; he will never leave you nor forsake you" (Deut. 31:6).

"Where are you?" he yelled as he stumbled into the house. I didn't know whether he was talking to my mama or me. At first, when Daddy went into a rage, he only talked funny, but he was loud and was mean to Mama. He called Mama names, made fun of her cooking, and laughed at the way she combed her hair. He yelled at her when she knocked over her glass of water and told her she was as bad as the kids. If we kids left something on the floor, he would tell Mama that she was the worst housekeeper he had ever seen. "Were you born in a barn?" he snarled. "Did you live in a pig's pen?"

He yelled at us to stay out of his way and acted like he was going to kick us if we didn't. We mostly stayed out of his way, in the other room or playing outside. Daddy never hugged or kissed us goodnight, but sometimes he allowed us to kiss him goodnight. I kept trying to be friends with him, but he just didn't want to be friends with me.

From the beginning of the physical abuse, Mama didn't want us to see her crying or hear Daddy knocking her into furniture or slapping her across the face. She didn't scream or cry. She didn't say bad words. I don't think she hit Daddy back because we didn't hear Daddy say anything about that when the yelling was going on. I didn't see Daddy hit Mama because we would be sitting quietly behind the door, afraid to come out. In the beginning, I didn't run to find a hiding place.

I don't remember being physically hurt when I was very little. I just remember being scared. At first, the physical abuse in the family didn't really occur too often, but as the months and years of marriage accumulated, more babies were born, Daddy's physical illness became worse, the use of alcohol increased, and the times of beating Mama grew closer together.

Before we were big enough to hide by ourselves, Mama helped us hide. I don't remember where others were hidden; I only remember where she put me. She hid me on top of pillows and quilts in the sweet-smelling cedar chest. She always hung part of the quilt out so I could breathe easier. My bed was comfortable, and the sounds were muffled as I fell asleep in my hiding place. A few years later, I helped my little sister into that same cedar chest, telling her to take a nap.

Whenever Daddy finally fell asleep, we would come out of our hiding places and run to see what Mama was doing. Mama would give each of us a quick hug and tell us to pray and get ready for bed.

> Now I lay me down to sleep,
> I pray the Lord my soul to keep;
> If I should die before I wake,
> I pray the Lord my soul to take.

Mama led us in this prayer nightly and sometimes even while she was hiding me. Sometimes I chanted the prayer over and over as if it were bringing me protection. I wasn't thinking about Daddy trying to kill me; I didn't even know what killing or dying really meant. But I knew the feelings of contentment and safety that came when we said the words of the prayer together or when I chanted or sang the words over and over in my mind.

THOUGHTS TODAY

I find peace now looking at that old cedar chest. Like me, it could tell many stories of happenings around its life. The top of the chest has loosened, and the feet are missing. The inside shelf doesn't move any more. Filled with memories, the chest has aged along with me.

Mama gave me the chest because I was the first one to sleep in it. Today, the chest is crammed with my personal family photos, certificates, awards, newspaper articles, and other documents collected over the years at school, camp, and church. But when I see it or touch it, I sense my mother's love.

My Prayer of Thanks

Dear Father,
Thank You for the peace I feel now when I remember the past. Thank You for taking away the nightmares and helping me to feel safe. You are truly my hiding place.

Thank You for the prayer that seemed to unite our family over the years as we got ready for bed in the evenings and for the mother who planted it so firmly in our hearts and mind. Amen.

Hiding in the Tent

"For in the day of trouble he will keep me safe in his dwelling; he will hide me in the shelter of his sacred tent and set me high upon a rock" (Ps. 27:5).

"Come, let's go make a tent," Mama cheerfully called out as we sat playing with our toys on the big rock outside. I was just a little over four years old when Mama fixed us a tent to play in underneath the crevice of a big rock going up the path toward the outhouse. The overhang of the rock made a shallow cave for little bodies. Mama tied a corner of a plastic table cloth to the bushes and put heavy rocks to hold the other ends down. She pushed in a pillow, Daddy's old army blanket, and a mason jar full of cool water from the outside spigot. She added soft toys that made no noise. The street light on Grove Street gave just enough light to see the outhouse and our back door. We loved it!

The hiding place was big enough for the three of us kids to play in when we were told, "Go." We didn't really mind being in our hiding place. We softly sang Sunday school songs, and my big sister—she was five—told long stories. They were always scary stories, but they did not seem as scary as when Daddy was beating Mama. We always stopped singing and never said a word if we heard a snap of a twig or a car coming up the Upper Street gravel road. We waited silently if we heard someone walking toward the outhouse. Most of the time, we fell asleep, safe in our tent in the middle of a long story.

When Daddy was acting up, Mama would sadly smile and just say, "Go," and we would run up the hill to our hiding place. If anyone saw us, they would think we were just going to the outhouse. We did not look back, and no one called out to us to stop. No one bothered us. The bushes covered the shallow opening, welcoming us to our play area, our story room, our secret cave, our camping tent, our special hiding place. We always remembered to say the prayer Mama taught us.

> "Now I lay me down to sleep,
> I pray the Lord my soul to keep;
> If I should die before I wake,
> I pray the Lord my soul to take."

We cuddled together under Daddy's army blanket, and my sister told us scary stories about witches casting spells and monsters hiding in closets. Sometimes we laughed at how scary the stories were supposed to be. It was dark outside our tent, but we still had the streetlight to make us feel safe. We could see monsters if they came walking up the hill. We could see witches flying in overhead. We felt safe. Sometimes, we asked if real monsters lived in the closets. My big sister said, "No, not when Daddy is around."

We never spent all night in our hiding place because as soon as Daddy fell asleep, Mama would go toward the outhouse, whispering, "Come out. Let's go home." We did not say anything about the tears on her face or bruises on her arms. We only saw Mama and felt her holding us close. She always said she was taking her sweet little babies back home.

THOUGHTS TODAY

I marvel that as preschool kids, we were able to stay quiet and hidden so long. I find it difficult to believe that we did not quarrel and fight over toys. However, I know even at that age, I would never have done anything to hurt my mama. And besides, we had all our stories bursting to come out of our vivid imaginations.

Mama encouraged us and expected us to obey. She praised us when we followed directions. Where did I find the courage to run to a hiding place when Mama was being beaten? The only thing I can think of is that I loved and trusted my mama. She would never tell me the wrong thing. So, when I heard, "Go," I ran. My sister ran. My brother ran.

My Prayer of Thanks

Dear Father,
Thank You for giving me to a Christian mother who loved You and put each of us in Your care. Thank You for helping me to not be greatly scarred by what I saw and heard as a child. Thank You for hiding places that were fun. Thank You for my sister, who entertained us with stories. Amen.

Mama Confronts Granny

"Rescue me from my enemies, Lord, for I hide myself in you" (Ps. 143:9).

The path on the other side of the outhouse led from our house to Granny's house. Granny loved our daddy very much. Granny always brought Daddy special meals because he was sick. His plate even had meat on it. She didn't bring Mama anything to eat. Mama was not sick. She didn't bring us anything to eat. We were not sick. We watched Daddy eating food we had never tasted or seen before. We wanted to taste that food, but we were not sick. Daddy always had milk to drink. Granny said he needed it more than us because he was sick. Sometimes I wanted to be sick.

We began going to Granny's house when she was at work and Grandpa was taking his nap. Sometimes, Daddy's youngest sister would give us a piece of light bread and bologna from the grocery store. Sometimes, she would give us a drink of RC. And if she really was pleased we were there, she would give us vanilla wafer cookies. With the yummy food, special drinks, a television to watch, and a young person giving us attention, we thought Granny's house would be a perfect place to hide from Daddy.

The next time Mama said, "Go," we ran up the hill, but instead of going to our hiding place, we kept going. We ran past our hiding place, past the outhouse, across the Upper St. gravel road, and up the many steps to Granny's house. Out of breath, we told Granny that Daddy was sick. We quickly explained that Daddy was yelling and calling Mama names. We told her Daddy slapped Mama if she said anything. Granny was not pleased with our report. Before we finished telling her why we were there, she grabbed my arm and turned me around. She hit my bottom over and over and over again. I didn't know what I did wrong. Then she hit my sister even harder. She angrily told us to never tell lies about our daddy again.

We were hiccupping with our crying. "Shut up," Granny yelled again. "You don't cry like that in my house," as she piled a plate with delicious-looking food. Granny had said the bad word in front of us. We got quiet. Granny walked us hurriedly down the many steps of the porch, across the Upper St. gravel road, past the outhouse, and back down the hill to our house. We didn't dare look in the direction of our hiding place.

Granny didn't even knock; she opened the door and walked right into our house. She told Daddy to sit down and have something to eat. Daddy quickly obeyed. Then she yelled at our surprised Mama and told her if she took better care of Daddy, he wouldn't be the way he was. She told Mama if she fixed better meals, Daddy wouldn't drink so much. She was in Mama's face, yelling the whole time. She didn't have to yell; we all could hear her. Mama didn't cry. Mama didn't say a word. She stood there just staring at Granny.

When Granny left, we ran to Mama and told her we were sorry that we ran up the hill to Granny's. When we told her that Granny had yelled at us and slapped our bottoms, Mama got quiet and walked us up the path to our tent. She told us to stay put. We didn't. We followed Mama from a short distance past the outhouse, up the hill, and across the Upper St. gravel road. This time, we did not climb the many steps to Granny's porch. We stood quietly underneath while Mama talked firmly to Granny.

Mama did not yell, but we could tell Mama meant business. She told Granny she could say anything and do anything to her that she wanted to, but she better not touch any of her kids again. Some of the words were muffled as we ran back across the Upper St. gravel road, past the outhouse, and down the path leading to our hiding place.

We never tried to hide at Granny's house again. We knew she would tell Daddy we were there. And if she saw us running up the hill to find our hiding place, she would send Daddy's sister to tell him where we were.

Even Grandpa could not be trusted to help us find a hiding place. He liked to touch us in a way that we didn't like. He liked to pinch us and shoot rubber bands at us. They really hurt. One time, Grandpa slapped Granny and then asked us if we wanted some. We didn't quite know what he meant, but we went home as fast as we could.

Aunt Louise said Grandpa used to beat our daddy until Daddy married Mama. She whispered she wanted to grow up so she could run away from home. She said the next time Grandpa hit her, she was getting out of there.

Aunt Louise loved Mama's sweet tea. Almost every day, she followed the path down the hill carrying an empty half-gallon jar to our house. Mama would fill the jar with her southern sweet tea. Sometimes, Aunt Louise helped us get dressed in the mornings. She liked to play with us, even though she was already fifteen years old. She walked with us to the little Church of the Nazarene on Sundays. We really liked her, but we would never tell her about our hiding place. She might tell Granny.

Thoughts Today

I realize now that Granny must have been overly concerned about her youngest son, who was so very, very sick. The doctors did not know how long her son could live with his lung problems. Each surgery removed parts of his lung and weakened his body. There were no medications that could have helped him breathe easier. Granny must have seen the worsening of his overall health and felt helpless.

Granny must have also been concerned that Mama, who married Daddy at sixteen, had small children to take care of constantly. She must have thought Mama knew very little about how to take care of someone seriously ill.

It's not that Granny disliked Mama so much but that she loved her son more.

Years later, Granny softened her view of Mama and her children. Daddy remained the priority, but we received candy for Christmas, and Mama received a scarf. Daddy received socks, shoes, pants, and a new shirt.

I don't know why we children were so obsessed with food in those days. I remember having enough to eat, but perhaps the variety of food was at a minimum, and desserts were not on the menu in the early years. Everything we ate was from scratch. We had mush, cornbread and beans with a ham bone, hot cornbread and milk, biscuits and milk gravy, biscuits and chocolate gravy, fried potatoes, potato salad, and occasionally, fried chicken. They remain my comfort food.

Our menu might have had poverty written all over it in the 1950s but would be on restaurant menus today. As soon as she was able, Mama raised chickens for eggs and meat. She even bought a nanny goat to give us fresh milk for cooking. Mama used every space in that rocky yard and hillside to plant vegetables to can. The chickens ran free as we chased them, and the goat jumped from the rocks to the rooftop to get away from us kids.

Mama would really be surprised to see that most of the huge rocks have been removed from that hillside, the trees are gone, and the outhouse has been torn down, but there is more space for her garden.

My Prayer of Thanks

Dear Father,
Thank You for working in the lives of all those who at first meant to cause us harm. Thank You for Granny, who learned to love us and love Mama in the best way she could. Help me to not have bad feelings for Granny being unable to love my mama more. Thank You for helping Mama to teach us to respect Granny and Grandpa.

Thank You for helping Mama to always have enough food for growing children. Thank You for giving her creative ways to plant vegetables on that rocky hillside. Amen.

Daddy's Special Medicine

"Stop drinking only water, and use a little wine because of your stomach and your frequent illnesses" (1 Tim. 5:23).

Daddy had a hard time breathing with only one lung. Sometimes, he would cough and spit up ugly green phlegm. We hated hearing Daddy gag as he coughed up the mucus from his lung. We hated to see him spit the phlegm in the same tin can he spit his tobacco and where he put his cigarette butts.

Mama changed his soiled bandages every day, explaining to each of us how to do it. We were fascinated with the hole in his back and didn't really understand when Mama talked about the loss of his lung and the continual drainage on that side of his back. She taught us to clap on Daddy's back, chest, or sides with a cupped hand in order to shake mucus loose from the lungs. Sometimes, Mama said to hit him lightly with the side of our hand and fingers. She liked it when he coughed and spit up the ugly mucus. I did not like it at all and tried not to gag.

Sometimes, Daddy would walk down Grove St. to Carter Massey's store on the corner. Daddy couldn't work, but he could sit entertaining customers who sat awhile outside and chatted to people walking by. Sometimes, Daddy ran the cash register while Carter straightened his goods. Everyone liked Daddy. Sometimes, we walked to the same store with Mama. Daddy told us we could share an RC or have a one-cent piece of candy. On special days, Daddy gave each of us four pieces of the one-cent strawberry or chocolate kit. On special days, when Daddy paid off our credit charges, we shared a Moon Pie and a Yoo-hoo drink. Daddy would add the cost to our new credit sheet that he would pay again next month. I liked that Daddy. Why didn't he stay the Daddy everyone liked?

In the evenings, Daddy would get a ride or walk to the police station near the Ft. Loudon bridge. We would sit outside on the steps of the jailhouse porch or in the rocking chairs. A police officer would measure out a shot of whiskey to help clear Daddy's lung. There was nothing else that could help—no medicines, no therapy. We watched Daddy laugh and the police officers laugh with him. I didn't know what was so funny, but I liked that Daddy. Sometimes, the police would give us a piece of gum, and we all laughed.

As Daddy signed the form for the medicine he had taken, he called us inside to look in the back where people stood behind bars. He told us that the jail is where very bad boys and girls go. I made a promise to myself to never be bad, no matter what Daddy did to me. I promised to always wave at the prisoners when we crossed the bridge. They might have had a bad daddy like I did.

Thoughts Today

Today, I feel sadness for that Daddy. I wish I could go back and tell him that cigarettes make his breathing worse. I would try to be more cheerful when it was my turn to wash away the drainage from the hole in his back. If I went back in time, I would smile when I changed Daddy's bandage. I would be more understanding when Daddy couldn't do physical things and play like other dads did. I would not complain so much when I was asked to rub or tap his back so the phlegm would break up and he could breathe easier. I know I would be more forgiving if I could just visit one more time. But I did not feel any empathy for Daddy back then. I did not like him all that much.

I always remembered to wave at the people looking through the bars as I went across the Loudon bridge. I taught my children to wave until the building was no longer there. Perhaps thinking of those women in the jail who may have been abused, I later became involved in women's prison ministries in Nashville. I told my story and they listened. As they stepped outside to line up for dinner, a few remained in the room for prayer.

My Prayer of Thanks

Dear Father,
Thank You for helping Daddy find the only medicine available at that time to clear his lung. Help those involved in discovering new medicines for lung disease to be able to find the finances and personnel needed for research.

Help me to have more empathy when I visit the sick or those in assisted living. Give me a stronger stomach and more patience with the sick. Help me remember to talk with those in prison as opportunities arise. Amen.

The Butcher Knife

"Our God is a God who saves; from the Sovereign Lord comes escape from death" (Ps. 68:20).

Sometimes, we were so interested in playing games that we paid little attention to adults and didn't hear Daddy getting angry until it was too late to leave the house. Daddy was looking for the butcher knife that Mama always kept hidden from us kids. It was long and had a thin, sharp blade. Daddy searched until he found the knife on top of the kitchen cabinet under a stack of towels. Daddy was already cursing and threatening Mama with the butcher knife before we even had a chance to hide.

I grabbed Sue, who seemed to follow me everywhere I went, and dragged her to the one and only closet. I pushed her scared and shaking body down behind me. I covered her up with the pile of clothes lying nearby. Daddy would not grab her if he found me first. I piled a quilt on top of me. I heard Daddy jerk back the closet curtains, but he couldn't see us squeezed way back in the darkness under the piles of the quilt and clothes. He couldn't see Barbara and Larry hiding under the bed. We were all safe. Daddy didn't see well when he had too much to drink. Mama said God was looking over us. Mama was always saying things like that.

Hiding in the house was not a good idea. Covering our heads and putting our hands over our ears did not stop us from hearing Mama cry out, "No, Ralph. Please stop." We could follow the sounds from room to room as Mama tried to get to a door leading outside to freedom. We heard Mama scream and Daddy laughing. It was not the laughing of the Daddy I liked.

Mama was still crying when we heard Daddy snoring. We slipped out of our hiding places and could see Mama had blood dripping from her head, even though she had wrapped a towel around her head and a handkerchief around her arm.

We were so excited when Mama said we were going to walk up a big mountain. We started up the hill, past the hiding place, and around the outhouse. Don't stop; keep walking up the hill; cross the Upper St. gravel road; pass Granny's house; keep climbing up the hill. Don't stop; follow the path. My feet hurt; keep climbing. We were breathing hard. Mama carried the little one. We were tired. Mama was tired. "Can't we sit on the rocks and rest?" "No, keep climbing." Mama's head is bleeding. Mama's arm is all red with blood. Keep walking. Mama didn't lead us in prayer. She didn't tell us stories. She didn't even sing songs as we walked along.

Mama cried when she saw the hospital. We cried when we saw Mama crying.

The nurses came running and took the little one out of Mama's arms, and they hugged us tightly. They gave us chocolate milk to drink. It was my first time to drink chocolate milk. I thought it was medicine because we were at the hospital. Mama told the nurses how she had fallen against a huge rock outside our house and hit her head and scraped her arm on the way to the outhouse. The nurse stitched Mama's head. She put clean bandages around both Mama's head and her arm. Mama did not look good. Her eyes were big and her face red as the nurse said, "You must be very careful when you are walking around rocks. You have children to think of now."

After the nurses were finished and Mama promised to be more careful where she walked, we started back down the hill to the path that led to Granny's house, that led across the Upper St. gravel road, down the hill, and past the outhouse. It was not so bad going down.

When we got to our hiding place, we rested. Mama told us to say our prayers.

"*Now I lay me down to sleep,*

*I pray the Lord my soul to keep;
If I should die before I wake,
I pray the Lord my soul to take."*

Mama let us sing very quietly, "Jesus Loves Me." Then Mama explained to us that she didn't really tell a lie to the nurse. She told us about the time she fell going up the hill and her head got cut deeply on a rock. She told us people might say bad things about us if they knew Daddy cut her with a butcher knife. She told us to never lie. I was a little bit confused.

From then on, Mama kept the butcher knife in another special hiding place. I could never find it, but a few times, Daddy still found the knife so he could chase Mama.

One day, the man cutting the weeds off the side of our hill found our hiding tent. He took all our play things to Mama. We needed another hiding place.

Thoughts Today

I do not think Mama would have ever directly lied to anyone. She was not that type of person. She never deliberately lied to manipulate others and receive some personal benefit. However, Mama deliberately omitted some truths in order to avoid conflict and hide the behavior of Daddy to our family members, neighbors, and friends. The cousins called it *Lambertism—the act of telling a half-truth or leaving out facts in order to protect someone.*

Charles H. Bacon Hospital was only a six-minute walk up the hill, but with preschool children and a hurt mother, it must have seemed much farther.

My Prayer of Thanks

Dear Father,
Thank You for helping Mama be a survivor, although she struggled through being slapped forcefully by Daddy's hands, being angrily beaten with his

fists, being stitched because of deep cuts from a butcher knife, and being scared as bullets went astray. Thank You for filling her heart with forgiveness toward a threatening and abusive husband and father.

Help me to be more forgiving toward those who directly and indirectly threaten me in my workplace and at home. Help me to tell the truth when someone abuses me. Amen.

Hiding under the Covers

"But understand this: If the owner of the house had known at what time of night the thief was coming, he would have kept watch and would not have let his house be broken into" (Matt. 24:43).

Sometimes, Uncle Shorty would drive Daddy to the veterans hospital in North Carolina. Daddy didn't go to the one in Florida or Walter Reed in Washington any more. Sometimes, Daddy might stay a few weeks for a surgery on his lung or go for a few days for a thorough checkup.

We liked it when Daddy was gone. We could sing loud and play rough. We could shout if we wanted; no more running to hide; no more worries about Mama getting hurt. For fun at night, we all slept in the same bed while Mama told us more stories of living on the farm in Tellico. She told us how her dad used to ask her, in front of all his friends, to roll his cigarette and light it for him. They would clap and give her a plug of tobacco if she rolled the cigarette and licked it just good enough to hold the papers together. She would give the tobacco to her brother in exchange for candy. Sometimes, she would roll cigarettes for the friends of her daddy and light their cigarettes for them, too. Mama thought that is why she started smoking regularly when she was six years old. Mama made us promise to never roll or light someone's cigarette.

Mama laughed as she talked about the green snake that once got onto the shiny linoleum floor in the eating room at Granny Baker's house. It slipped and slid all over the place but just could not make it to the door. Everyone seeing the snake was laughing and screaming. Finally, Granny

Baker swept the snake right out the door. We felt cozy and safe, listening to Mama's memories.

But one night, our story time was interrupted. I thought Daddy had come home early. I could hear him cursing and singing loudly. He stumbled up the two little steps to the front door. He banged over and over on the door, yelling to be let in. For some reason, Mama did not let Daddy in. Finally, he broke the lock and pushed open the front door. We covered our heads. The man walked straight through the two-room house to the kitchen.

The man sounded like Daddy, but it was not Daddy. It was too late to run. It was too late to get under the bed. There was no other hiding place except under the covers. We heard Mama give an almost silent whisper of "Shhh."

The stranger stumbled over the chairs and accidentally ran into the table. He laughed uncontrollably. We could smell him across the room. We recognized the smells. He smelled dirty and sweaty and drenched with alcohol. We could hear him as he opened the refrigerator and knocked things around before he slammed the door shut. He banged against cabinets, forcibly opening and closing the doors as he tried to find whatever he was looking for. He bumped into the coal bucket and knocked black pieces of coal and coal dust all over Mama's clean floor. We didn't know what he wanted.

Then we heard the footsteps come near the bed. My big sister's stories were coming alive as we imagined—the man was taking the first step toward our bed, taking the second step, taking the third step. We made no sounds and held our eyes tightly closed with our heads covered. What was he doing? Was he looking at me? Was he going to jerk the covers off the bed? Was he going to hurt us? The man finally turned and walked clumsily out the door and down the two steps to the street only a few feet away.

After a few minutes, Mama got up, relocked the door the best she could, and placed a chair under the door knob. It was the first time I ever saw my mama cry and cry. She said God was looking over us. She was always talking about God when something bad happened. She held us close and told us to say our prayers:

> "Now I lay me down to sleep,
> I pray the Lord my soul to keep;
> If I should die before I wake,
> I pray the Lord my soul to take."

The next night, Uncle James came to stay with us and would always come whenever Daddy was gone with Uncle Shorty.

Thoughts Today

The two-room house on Grove Street was built in 1910. Today, people would call the 690-square-foot residence a *Tiny* house. A stranger could walk through the entire house in two minutes, but it must have seemed forever to the little girl under the covers.

I don't remember Mama ever praying out loud for me. But she said she prayed for me and all her children every day. She did lead us in a mealtime prayer and the nighttime prayer, sometimes even during the day.

> "Now I lay me down to sleep,
> I pray the Lord my soul to keep;
> If I should die before I wake,
> I pray the Lord my soul to take."

Mama did not teach us the prayer because she was afraid of dying. She did not teach us the prayer to make us afraid. Mama wanted us to understand that God was our protector. She wanted us to know that wherever we were hiding, God was right there with us, watching and listening. She wanted us to know we were safe.

My Prayer of Thanks

Dear Father,
Thank You for keeping my family safe from those who would have harmed us. Thank You for a mother who remained calm during a time of danger.

Thank You for helping Daddy to be able to make the long trips to the doctors and hospitals where they experimented with ways to make his life easier with one lung. Amen.

A Secret Club House

"The name of the Lord is a fortified tower; the righteous run to it and are safe" (Prov. 18:10).

Grandpa's brother had a lot of used cars, trucks, and piles of all kinds of parts in his salvage junkyard beside our house. We were not allowed to be there since it was a place of business. But my little cousin said we could have a secret clubhouse in one of the broken-down cars if we didn't tell her daddy. We walked around most of the cars, looking inside them and checking for doors that opened and closed. Finally, in the middle of the junkyard, we found a dark blue car that was just a little rusty. The old car sat on the ground with no tires and no front, but inside, it still had front and back seats. We cleaned the inside the best we could. It was beautiful.

We carried Kool-Aid, a few toys, and our hiding place blanket and pillow to our newly established clubhouse. My cousin brought her blanket and sandwiches for all of us made from bread, mayonnaise, and lettuce. As we turned the squeaky steering wheel, we imagined we were driving to faraway places. Our meal was the best we had eaten in a long while. We loved our secret place, but I had a special plan for our clubhouse. I made my cousin promise that she would never tell anyone about our secret clubhouse. She never told anyone, not her sister June, not even her parents, but I told Mama that I had found a new hiding place.

A few days later, Daddy walked into the house carrying a gun and making threats. Where did he find a gun? Who gave it to him? Did he buy it? Where did he find money to buy a gun? Did he borrow the gun? Why would someone loan it to him? We had no answers.

Finding a Hiding Place

When Mama said, "Go," we ran out the back door and into the jungle of old cars and trucks. We remembered how to get to the clubhouse, but there was only one street light far away, making it difficult at first to recognize our ugly car. We finally found the old rusty thing and climbed into our secret hiding place. We lay weeping on the faded upholstered seats that had broken wires sticking up. We hated this place. We could hear Mama yelling at Daddy to put the gun down. Would our tears ever stop? We wondered if the neighbors and Granny could hear the gunshots and Mama crying, or if they were just ignoring the situation. The tired old car trembled with our tears.

Much later, Mama climbed into our clubhouse. Mama was alive. She brought us more blankets and water and leftover cornbread. For a special treat, she brought us Vienna sausages. We were so excited to get this rare surprise. Mama rubbed our feet and calmly talked to us. Daddy had fallen asleep. She had hidden the gun. All was well.

We stayed awhile in the beautiful car that night. It was so peaceful seeing Mama behind the shiny steering wheel. Sitting up straight and holding tightly to the steering wheel, Mama predicted Daddy might buy us a car soon. We loved this car. She told us stories about riding in a car that had two rows of seats in the back. Mama shared childhood experiences about helping her dad on the farm and how she rode on tractors, horses, and mules and in the backs of timber trucks going to market. She explained how her brothers used to help her jump on the moving box car when it slowed down near the crossroad. Then they helped her jump off when she got to the town so she could go to school. We would come back the next time to this wonderful car.

As usual, we prayed before we left our hiding place.

> "Now I lay me down to sleep,
> I pray the Lord my soul to keep;
> If I should die before I wake,
> I pray the Lord my soul to take."

We walked home that night, thinking that our mama was the bravest woman in the world. We were safe. We had found another hiding place. My cousin never told and soon forgot over the years that we even had a secret clubhouse in her dad's junkyard.

Thoughts Today

Now the junkyard and the hiding place are gone, but the house we lived in still stands. Glancing at the house as I drive by seventy-two years later, I wonder if it is possible for the sounds of the past, that of uncontrollable crying and stinging slaps one after another, can combine with all the other sounds of abuse. Did the house absorb the sounds of gunshots? I wonder if the soft whimpering and sniffling of children in hidden places are still weaving in and out of the corners of that little house.

Do we have an unused sense that can see and hear emotions? I wonder if emotions could be heard, would we hear hatred and anger and overwhelming fear still hovering over the house? I wonder if the new owners can feel and sense the sounds if they really listened.

But surely, after we moved out, the new renter saw that we had lived there. Did they cover up the puddles of salty tear drops and blood stains on the floor? Did they fix the broken door? Do they know where to hide their butcher knife? Do they even know where to hide?

My Prayer of Thanks

Dear Father,
Thank You for taking away my anxiety when I hear sounds that remind me of physical abuse. Thank You for helping me not to yell and lose control when I hear firecrackers or gunshots. Help me to enjoy the fireworks.

Help me to be alert to others who may be reacting to sounds because of what has happened or is happening in their lives. Amen.

Hiding in the Coal Shed

"It will be a shelter and shade from the heat of the day, and a refuge and hiding place from the storm and rain" (Isa. 4:6).

We were excited to move to the second project, as we proudly called the housing area for World War II veterans. We had inside water in both the kitchen and bathroom. No more running up the hill to the outhouse; we had a toilet that flushed. We had a water heater. There was a big bath tub where we could take baths. No more going to the outside spigot for water; no more boiling water and filling the metal galvanized tub for a bath.

But best of all about our move was that we needed no hiding place. Daddy was so happy with our move that he didn't drink heavily any more. And besides, he could no longer walk to the jailhouse to sign up for a shot of whiskey. We were in no rush to find hiding places, but we did look, just in case the old Daddy came back. There was a closet in each of the three rooms and one with shelves in the hallway. There was the dirty old coal shed with small pieces of coal and a hot attic with no floor or windows. There were two trees with lots of leaves covering thick limbs and lots of hedges lining the edges of the front yard. There was a new, used couch to hide behind and new beds to hide under.

Our new house on Huffland Drive was surrounded by similar houses with children our ages. They played in the streets until the street lights came on, and then everyone disappeared into their own homes. So, we learned to do the same thing.

We had the responsibility of carrying coal into the house every day until Daddy had someone put a gas heater in the floor of the hallway. We no longer needed to use coal to heat the house. We had found a new play area in the old coal shed.

We swept and washed the shed over and over. It seemed we always came out black, our clothes, our hair, and our arms and legs. Its dust and ash seeped under our nails and into our ears. Mama was not pleased and gave an ultimatum that we could not get that dirty again.

After that, we took our outer clothes off and cleaned the shed. My brother sprayed water in until the water came out gray, but not black. We used flour and water to paste newspaper and pictures we had colored at school and church on the walls and ceiling. Our new clubhouse was beautiful. The Sunday school papers seemed to lighten the room, even if the newspaper ink kept getting on our skin just like the coal. Mama gave us a flashlight. We carried our faithful army blanket into the mostly clean shed. It was the best hiding place yet. Larry put a lock on the inside of the door and fixed the outside lock to close but not lock the door.

Daddy bought a beautiful used car on credit. He took us all for a ride. There were six kids in the family now. Mama held the baby and rode up front with Daddy. The five of us sat in the back seat. He stopped at a gas station and bought us candy on credit. He brought out a brown paper bag for himself. We did not recognize what was in the bag. We were so happy with our new house and new car. We didn't like pushing the car up the hill, but we loved having a car. We thought we were almost rich.

The next night, we heard our brand-new used car pull into the driveway. It stopped so quickly, gravel hit the side of the house. We peeped under the window shade. It was Daddy, and he looked like the old Daddy from our other house.

We gathered our things and ran out the back door to our shed, our new safe place. We cracked opened the door so we could hear the voices better. When Daddy got quiet, we went back in the house. We were filthy dirty with coal dust when we got back into the house, but Mama didn't say anything this time.

My older sister never played or hid in the shed. She stayed in one of the closets, holding the baby. It seemed like she always wanted to take care of Mama's babies. On good days, my sister would comb my hair and put it in pigtails. She loved fixing hair.

When my sister refused to hide in the shed, we no longer could depend on her stories that helped us forget what was happening around us. I became the storyteller when my older sister was not around, but I never told scary stories. I told stories from the Bible or books I was reading at school. I told stories about someone leaving a million dollars with Mama like a show on TV, and we would pass time slowly discussing how we would spend the money. We usually ended by saying that we were going to buy a washing machine so Mama wouldn't need to use the ringer washer anymore. We knew we would have to keep it a secret like the man on TV said, but we also knew we were good at keeping secrets. We were happy in our hiding place because all our toys were there, and we could tell stories. But most of all, we were happy because Daddy didn't find us.

Thoughts Today

When we lived in the old Grove St. house, I accidentally inhaled coal oil—kerosene—by drinking from a coke bottle where the kerosene had been stored to build a fire later in the coal stove. I spent a few nights in the hospital. I was treated with oxygen support.

Then in our new Huffland Dr. house, while cleaning and spending many hours in the coal shed, more damage was probably done to my lungs. The coal dust from my hiding place probably caused some scarring of my lungs. I am on oxygen 24/7. The results of hiding may have affected me in more ways than just in physical beatings and emotional abuse.

I still give a chuckle when I remember the 1950s TV series, *The Millionaire*, where a multi-billionaire gives away $1 million apiece to persons he has never met. The show tells how their lives were changed. We thought it was real people who received the monies. It was our favorite show. We made lists of what we would buy and looked up prices in the

Sears catalog so we would know how much money would be left. When someone new knocked at our door, we all stopped what we were doing, in hopes that *The Millionaire* man was at the door.

My Prayer of Thanks

Dear Father,
Thank You for giving us a better and safer place to live in through the low-rent veteran housing units in the second project. Thank You for helping Daddy to get the car that was so needed. You have been so good to us as a family, even if there have been difficult times.

Help me to always be grateful for a good childhood surrounded by friends my own age. Thank You for helping us not to tell friends about Daddy so they kept coming to visit. Thank You that we had many friends who enjoyed being at the Lambert's house. Amen.

Stuffing Sue in the Couch

"Rescue me from my enemies, Lord, for I hide myself in you" (Ps. 143:9).

Sometimes, it got too cold in the shed. And no matter what we did to clean it, we came out blackened by the coal dust left behind. I knew by looking at Mama that I needed to find a new and better hiding place.

Mama got a job plucking feathers at the chicken company. When Daddy drove Mama to work, I tore the hole bigger on the back of the upholstered couch. We had kept our pet squirrel there, so I knew it had lots of space inside with the padding pulled out. We jerked up the cloth hanging down the back of the couch. We tore out lots of stuffing. We hid all the stuffing in a brown grocery bag in case Mama didn't like our idea and told us to put the stuffing back. Both Sue and Linda were so tiny; they could fit in the hole, but my brother and I were just too big.

We heard Daddy's car pull up in the driveway. The doors squeaked and scraped the hedges growing nearby. We looked at each other. It was time to hide in our new places around the house.

I pushed Sue into the hole in the back of the couch. There was just barely enough space for her. Sue did not like the new hiding place at all. Her knees came out some, but I could pull the back cover down over her. She said the padding itched her, and the coils of wire were sticking into her back. I knew Daddy would not be able to find her in the couch as long as she was quiet and didn't fall out. Barbara took little Linda and Jerry with her. Larry was always gone somewhere in the neighborhood. We knew he would see Daddy's car, stay away, and be safe.

Since I was too big to hide inside the couch, I lay as flat as I could between the couch and the wall. I could hear Daddy walking throughout the house. I heard the steps coming closer. He must have noticed that the couch had been moved out a little way from the wall. His steps came closer and closer. Soon, I felt a flyswatter hitting me back-and-forth, back-and-forth all over my head and back, until I came out running for the door. Somehow, I got away, and Sue was safe, still stuffed in the back of the couch. I would come back later when Daddy fell asleep or Mama came home.

Daddy seemed to like using the flyswatter on our backs and legs, but this time, he had hit my head so much, my ears were ringing, and the tops of my ears were bleeding. Our neighbor saw my blood-stained ears as I hid behind the hedges on her side of the bushes. She asked if I needed some bandages. I smiled and told her I was fine. I explained that I had hurt my ears when I was playing "Kick the Can" and hid in the hedges a few nights before. I politely smiled again, said goodbye, and walked away. I really had no place to go, so I headed up the hill toward Welch Avenue. I stayed in the shadows as I slipped beside Harrell's house to the empty field between the first and second projects. No one called out to me, so I headed to the drainage pipe in the gulley. It was dark in the gulley. I sat there until the street lights came on.

THOUGHTS TODAY

The gully has since been filled in, and storage buildings cover the area. There is no pipe to sit on, no shortcut to run through to get away from Daddy. I wonder where kids in the project hide now. I wonder if they have to go inside when the street lights come on.

We did not tell friends or neighbors, teachers or pastors, or anyone we met anything bad that happened in our family. Mama would say something like, "Don't air our dirty laundry so the neighbors can see it." So, we never told anything that might have damaged our family's reputation. We weren't protecting Daddy; we were protecting Mama.

By the way, I never really told a lie to our neighbor that time about my ears. I did scratch my ears, and they did bleed a little bit while hiding in the hedges during a game of "Kick the Can." It was just a case of *Lambertism*, *a half-lie to protect the reputation of the family.*

Mama made us put all the stuffing back in the couch, but it seemed to never feel the same. A year later, Daddy purchased a new Danish couch on credit from Greer's Hardware downtown. It had wooden legs with pillows to place against the slats on the back and pillows to sit on. There were no places to hide behind or under it.

My Prayer of Thanks

Dear Father,

Thank You for taking care of me and keeping me from great harm at the gulley and on the pipe going across the rock and tiny stream below. Thank You for Your protection.

Thank You for a neighbor who cared enough to ask if she could help when she observed that I was hurt. I don't remember anyone else offering to help in any way. Thank You for helping me to be strong and not tell of family matters. Amen.

Holding On for Dear Life

"For you have been my refuge, a strong tower against the foe" (Ps. 61:3).

After the beating with the flyswatter, I didn't hide behind the couch any more. I hid in the living room closet behind the suitcase of pictures and under the winter quilts and blankets. I was safe. But one time when he opened the closet door, Daddy remembered to look under the quilts and blankets. He jerked them up and threw them on the floor outside the closet. I didn't know what to do because he was blocking my escape.

Daddy had promised Mama he would not use a flyswatter, but that didn't stop Daddy from using his belt. As he pulled his belt through the loops, it looked like a whip slicing through the air. He hit my sore ears and bruised my back as I tried to get by him. He kicked me in the stomach as I crawled to the door. When Daddy finally got tired and started falling against the chair and the wall, I made my escape and ran from the house.

I had no idea where to go. The streetlights were on and the rule was to be home. With no place to go, I climbed the tree in our front yard. I held on tight to the place where the trunk and the biggest limb came together. Eventually, I cried myself to sleep. Later, I heard Mama calling my name. By this time, the streetlights had been on for a long time. I climbed down the tree, half-falling and half-sliding, crying out of control. My arms and legs were scratched from holding on to the tree trunk. I was covered with mosquito bites. My ears were bleeding again, and my back had big whelps. I held on to Mama as I cried and told her what Daddy had done. For some reason, I told her I forgot to say my prayers before I fell asleep. Mama said God already heard my prayers.

Mama and I walked into the quiet house. Daddy was sound asleep in his chair. My brothers and sisters lay on the floor and couch watching the black-and-white television program. Mama called the police; she didn't care who was listening on the party line this time. Mama was angry. She explained everything, but they didn't come and talk to Daddy. She told them Daddy was now hitting the kids, but they didn't come and take Daddy away. Instead, they told her they had more important things to do than answer every problem between a man and his wife.

Thoughts Today

Mama must have been hurt and disappointed when the police did not come, but that was the way society handled domestic violence back then—simply ignore the complaint. The man was the authority figure, especially in the home. Whatever he said or did was considered a part of his responsibility in maintaining his home. He was to be obeyed. He knew what was best. The church supported the culture fully. The woman was to be submissive and obey her husband. The husband was the head of his wife.

I have often been upset with the police for not coming to our aid. I realize now, the police were not really at fault. They had been trained to not respond to Mama's call or anyone who needed help if it was a domestic complaint. They were just doing their job.

I have often wondered what, if any, damage was done to my stomach. Why, when I feel anxiety or threatened, do I cover or hug my stomach tightly?

I remember how obedient all the kids were when the streetlights came on. Everyone knew the rules. If it was a warm summer night, we might get permission to sit on the porch and talk to neighbors across the street or next door, but we had to be home when the streetlights came on.

MY PRAYER OF THANKS

Dear Father,
Thank You for helping voters pass laws regarding physical abuse that provided training for police officers. Thank You for church leaders who are teaching the correct biblical meaning of submissiveness and male authority.

Help me to be alert to those around me who are being abused. Help me offer to them a means of coping or a way of escape. Amen.

Running Out of Places to Hide

"But the Lord said to him, 'Peace! Do not be afraid. You are not going to die'" (Judg. 6:23).

"Where are you?" he unexpectedly called out. We had no time to run for a safe hiding place. We slid under the bed as fast as we could. All three of us held our breaths as we watched his feet coming closer to the bed. We heard his loud grunt as he knelt and sneaked a look under the bed. His face momentarily disappeared as we heard his belt sliding from his pants, then the loud grunt again as he lay flat on the floor. Then, using his long black belt like a whip, he slashed out toward his children, going back-and-forth, back-and-forth across our heads and bodies. We escaped one by one, running to the door. Then, laughing wickedly, Daddy would chase us out the front door; while another one of us would escape and go out the back door, looking for a safe place to hide.

Sometimes we laughed and laughed as we ran, but it was never because we were having a good time. We laughed to make the neighbors think we were just playing games with our daddy. We laughed to keep from crying. We laughed because we didn't want Daddy to know we were that scared of him.

He yelled, "Where are you?" as he slammed doors and shoved furniture out of his way. He seemed to have superpowers when he had been drinking. Hidden in the back of the living room closet, I lay over the top of my baby sister. I thought Daddy would not catch us there. He rarely looked in the dark corners under blankets, but he guessed where we were and pulled the blanket off me. Using a rolled-up newspaper, he hit me wherever he could reach. I did not run this time. I did not want to escape. My sister was too little to understand what was happening. I could feel her angrily hitting my back and kicking underneath me. She wanted me off, but I didn't leave until Daddy's arms got tired, and he went to rest or look for another victim. When my little sister came out of the closet, she was crying almost out of control. She didn't understand. She hit me over and over. She didn't want to play with me anymore. She never let me hide her again.

I wanted to run away from home. I imagined and mentally practiced packing things to take with me. I got one of my sisters involved in packing things to take when we would run away. One week, we packed clothes; the next week, we packed water and food. As we rode in the car with Mama and Daddy, we watched for empty or abandoned houses. After several trips to Tellico, we found the one we would run off to. There were streetlights along the road and a cow trough nearby with a water pump. There were no houses close by. There was a door and windows for security. The house had not been painted for a long time. No one lived there or cared about it. It was perfect.

It was a long way to the abandoned house, so we practiced walking through the woods and finding a place to camp out. We walked to the creek and practiced catching crawfish and frogs to think about cooking and eating when we had no food.

I knew we needed money to live on. We sold the local newspaper to relatives and neighbors. We could keep a nickel from every ten-cent newspaper sold. With my friend Ramona and the help of her mother, we weaved and sold hot pads made with cotton loops and a metal frame for ten cents each. We borrowed sugar from Mama and sold glasses of Kool Aid at the corner for a nickel. We charged five cents for children and ten cents for adults in the neighborhood to sit on Daddy's army blanket and watch our Saturday shows. We advertised dog tricks, magic acts, acrobats, and songs. Both children and adults clapped loudly after each show, but we didn't make much money.

We wanted to run away; however, the money did not come in as quickly as we had thought it would. I was filled with questions. When would the time be right, and where would I run to? And how could I take my little sister? Where would we be safe? I was afraid to run.

THOUGHTS TODAY

The bruises from the newspaper rarely showed, and we never shared what happened with relatives, teachers, or friends. The bruises were our secrets. If our neighbors knew, they never said anything. If our relatives knew, they kept quiet. The police knew, but they never did anything.

Strange that our house became a favorite place for neighbors, friends from school, and cousins to visit. Strange that our yard was a place to gather and play *Red Rover, Dodge Ball, Red Light-Green Light or Mother, May I?* Somehow, we siblings always knew when Daddy would be sleeping it off, spending time at the American Legion, or going to a doctor's appointment. No one ever knew our dad had alcohol use disorder.

Enough money never came in at one time, and I was unable to run away from home with my sister Sue like I promised. Children threaten to run away all the time and don't mean it, but I meant to run away. My sister, who is now an older adult, still reminds me that I never ran away with her. She remembers the house we had planned to run to. She won't let me forget, though I have told her I am sorry for my failure many times. Even today, as I write this memory, we passed an empty run-down house on the corner near my home. While one sister said, "That would be a good house to flip," my sister Sue said, "We could have run away and lived there.

There were some unexpected effects of planning to run away. We learned how to plan and pack for a trip. We learned how to be resourceful in making and saving money. Surprisingly, we even learned to expand the selling of local newspapers to our own customers on specific routes.

My Prayer of Thanks

Dear Father,
Thank You for a childhood full of fun and lots of friends surrounding our house. Thank You for giving me such a good friend to share my adventures with. Thank You for helping me to develop a good relationship with my brothers and sisters as adults, despite my failures as a child.

Help me to be alert and approach children who say they want to run away from home. Help me to ask the right questions and find out if they really need help, and if they do need help, give me wisdom to know what to do. Amen.

A Picnic in the Cemetery

"Do not let your hearts be troubled. You believe in God; believe also in me. My Father's house has many rooms; if that were not so, would I have told you that I am going there to prepare a place for you? And if I go and prepare a place for you, I will come back and take you to be with me that you also may be where I am" (John 14:1–3).

Sometimes Mama was very creative in getting safely away from Daddy. One time, when Daddy arrived at home, we all tiptoed quietly out the back door. We walked to the cemetery on Steekee Street about a half mile away. The gate to the cemetery was locked, but at the far end near Ward Street, the cement block fence was even with the lawn on the other side. We entered easily by climbing the short fence and found a shady spot way back from the street in an area with no graves. Mama really surprised us. She had brought fried chicken, light bread, and a big jar of Cherry Kool-Aid. She had even brought a plastic table cloth, some plastic glasses, and a wet washcloth to wash our hands. Everything was so nice and peaceful. There was no yelling or shouting. There was no slapping or punching. Daddy was home, sleeping it off.

After we ate, we played running and jumping games and spent time reading the letters and numbers on the tombstones. We played the duck game when a car passed by. When Mama said "Quack, quack," we got down on the ground and didn't say a word until the car had passed. Then we got to waddle like a duck. Even Barbara played the game.

Mama told us stories about the people who had died and were buried there. She shared stories about the people whose names were engraved on the tombstones. She asked us if we could guess why they had a happy family. We always came up with an answer that mentioned, "because no one had to find a place to hide." I thought she knew all the families in the cemetery.

I felt so happy in the cemetery surrounded by so many good families. I found that cemeteries were not scary at all; they were a wonderful place to hide. Mama talked about dying and going to heaven. She told us about mansions, lots of food to eat, and angels walking around. She talked about Jesus and how much He loved children. She asked us to describe what we thought heaven looked like. Then she reminded us to pray our nighttime prayer:

> *"Now I lay me down to sleep,*
> *I pray the Lord my soul to keep;*
> *If I should die before I wake,*
> *I pray the Lord my soul to take."*

After a while, Mama told us to lie down on the warm, shiny stones or on the picnic cloth and rest. Mama was tired, but she didn't sleep. She kept a watch over us and sometimes hummed or sang a song.

I fell asleep thinking what a wonderful place heaven must be. She said to be nice to one another so we would get to go there. She made heaven sound like a place I wanted to go and stay there forever.

When we woke up, it was already dark, and the streetlights were on. Mama took us the long way home where there were streetlights. Curious, or perhaps nosy, neighbors would call out, "Where you been, Ms. Lambert?" "Why ya'll out so late, Ms. Lambert?" Mama waved and spoke her greetings with some of the neighbors still sitting on their rocking chairs on their front porches. But Mama never told them about our special picnic place. She never said why we were walking home after dark under the streetlights.

THOUGHTS TODAY

In one of my graduate classes, the professor discussed scenario-based learning. Scenarios are ways to help learners find solutions to a real problem. For instance, some of us kids kept coming in late long after the streetlights were on. Mama wanted to make sure we all knew to come in earlier, so she asked questions and made up a story with lots of endings. She would ask: "Could they see the streetlights?" "What were they doing?" "Why were they late?" "Can they be on time?" "Should they be punished?" Telling all the endings to the story helped us be creative and to remember to be on time.

Today, we call Mama's stories scenarios. We use scenarios, too, when something unexpected happens such as seeing a reckless driver or hearing a child crying in the grocery store or why the driver in the car beside us isn't smiling. We make up stories about why they act the way they do. I think we got our scenario skills from Mama.

MY PRAYER OF THANKS

Dear Father,
Thank You for a mother who planted the idea of heaven in my mind. In a few more years or even sooner, I will be coming to be with You. Help me to witness more to others, so they, too, can have their homegoing.

Thank You for a creative mother who knew so much for a woman under thirty with a third-grade education and six kids. Help me to be creative with children who are afraid, so that they, too, may feel safe. Amen.

Driving across the Loudon Bridge

"The Lord will fight for you; you need only to be still" (Exod. 14:14).

Daddy fell asleep very early, and Mama told us to quickly get in the car. She knew Daddy might wake up soon. She brought pillows and blankets and piled them around us. We stopped at *Carter Massey's* and charged chips and drinks and candy. She did not tell him where we were going. He was Daddy's friend and would tell him where we were. Carter would never tell Daddy we were going to the movies because everyone knew Mama couldn't drive across the Loudon Bridge.

When we got in the car, Mama told us to sit down and be very, very quiet. Mama really was going to drive across the Loudon Bridge. Mama was scared. We were scared. The bridge was narrow, and we could feel the bridge shaking as we drove across. We were quiet, and no semi-trucks came our way. Finally, we felt the last thump as we drove off the bridge. We were safe.

We made it to Cole's Drive-in Theater. Mama told all of us to get down and hide. Mama only had enough money to pay twenty-five cents for the car and twenty-five cents for one person. Later, Mama told us that kids were free that night. All six kids were free. Ha, ha, such a funny mama. She had tricked us all. We sat for a while on the army blanket outside and ate Mama's fried chicken. Some of us lay on top of the hood of the car until we got sleepy. Larry was too big to climb in the back window area to sleep, so Jerry inherited the window. Sue and Linda were getting too big to lie on either side of the big hump in the floor in front of the back seat. Until this night, I could stretch my legs out and sleep all by myself, but now I had to share my seat with Larry and Sue. Eventually, I climbed to the floor where I would not be kicked. Barbara slept with Mama and Linda in the front seat.

That night in the dark area of the outdoor movie was the best hiding place ever. We were the last ones to leave the theater grounds after the second show. I don't think we watched the movies; I don't even remember the names of those in the movies, but just being with Mama was fun. It was the last time I remember we went as a family to the drive-in movies.

Either because Mama was afraid of Daddy or afraid of driving back over the bridge in the dark, we did not go home that night. We parked in the trees along the highway across from the movie theater.

We all slept well that night. The sun was shining brightly, and it was nearing the time for *Carter's* to open when Mama started the car the next morning. We folded our blankets and combed our hair with our hands. And once again, Mama drove the car across the Loudon Bridge.

Thoughts Today

The drive-in remained our favorite hiding place of all time. The church was boycotting movies, so Mama told us to never say anything about going there, but today I told it all!

Mama was not the only one who didn't like to cross the river using the Loudon Bridge. The Loudon Bridge was narrow (ten feet wide). Sometimes we had to pull the mirrors in or back up to let a semi-truck come across. The bridge shook as a vehicle went across. We always had a joke that when the bridge needed repairs, the county would paint it a different color to hold it together. Since then, the old bridge has been replaced by a newer bridge that is not so scary.

My Prayer of Thanks

Dear Father,
Thank You for sending us a brave mother who set an example of Christian living for all of us. Thank You for a mother who, during my early years, made life an adventure, not a life of running from threats and fear.

Help me to observe those around me who might be running from danger. Help me not to be hesitant in asking if they need help. Amen.

Learning When to Hide

"For the Spirit God gave us does not make us timid, but gives us power, love and self-discipline" (2 Tim. 1:7).

As secret hiding places disappeared and new ones were difficult to get to quickly, we all learned better when to hide. We could hear the car pull in the driveway and the loose gravel spitting the side of the house as the car came to a quick stop. We could hear the screeching of the car door and its loud slam after Daddy stumbled out onto the ground. We could easily hear him mumbling and cursing as he walked up the path and climbed the four steps to the front porch. We listened as he always fell against the door frame while he entered the house, slamming the screen door, then the wooden door behind him. He always waited a few minutes to listen for the TV, the radio or someone whispering before yelling for one of us to come.

Whose name would he remember to call out? How long would it take him to fall asleep tonight? The questions wouldn't stop swimming around in my head. Would he use his belt or the flyswatter that was always kept beside his favorite chair? Or would he roll up the newspaper he had brought back from the American Legion meeting? Would he demand for one of us to go break a switch off the bushes outside?

We each hoped Daddy would ask us to break a switch from the hedges outside because after escaping, we would not come back inside the house. We would have the opportunity to run somewhere and hide. We liked it when Daddy would then send one of the others out to find the person who didn't return because then that person had the opportunity to run away, too. If Daddy wasn't thinking well, sometimes three or four of us might escape while his mind was on someone bringing a switch from the hedges outside.

Pay attention. Listen to the car pull in. Hear the gravel sliding and the door squeaking. Listen to the falling up the steps and the slamming of the door. Run out the back door or hide in the house. Don't make a sound. Daddy's home. Know where to run. Know where to hide. Keep the routine.

Thoughts Today

Actually, I think hiding as a child helped us develop special skills. Our listening skills improved as we listened for the car to pull in the driveway. We learned to be creative in finding places to hide. Accuracy of quick movements increased as we tried to escape Daddy's reach with the flyswatter, the belt, or newspapers he carried. We learned to run fast.

Making up scenarios to tell neighbors, teachers, and even ourselves in order to hide truths about our home life became a way of life and taught us to tell stories to entertain, become better readers and writers at school, and express ourselves in small and large groups. But we would never out and out lie, especially to an adult. God would not like that.

Today, when I drive on a gravel road or pull into a gravel driveway and hear gravel hitting the sides of the car, I think of Daddy. A slight shiver sometimes goes across my shoulders, but then I remember I am safe. All is well.

Every negative thing that happened to me, God turned it into something good. I have corrected my children without hitting them. I taught them that looking for hiding places was only a game. I encouraged them to love and obey their elders.

Daddy always spoke highly of the American Legion where he served as chaplain one year. I think he finally found the respect he needed from fellow veterans who knew his struggles after returning from the war.

My Prayer of Thanks

Dear Father,

Thank You for turning the negatives of my life into positives. Thank You that the physical abuse never became more violent. Thank You for making me into a strong and loving mother, just like my mama.

Thank You for providing Daddy the opportunity to be accepted by the veterans at the American Legion, who gave him some help with his problems of alcohol use. Help me to be a help to others when I see them struggling. Amen.

The Ugliest Doll in the World

"Take delight in the Lord, and he will give you the desires of your heart" (Ps. 37:4).

Christmas was coming, I wanted more than the usual jacks and hair pins. I wanted something special. Usually, I wanted something to do with sports, but this year, I had a big secret. I wanted a beautiful baby doll. I wrote a letter to Santa, and Mama and I carried the letter down to Mr. Amburn at the post office to mail. I tried to be good. I tried not to argue with my brothers and sisters. I tried to clean my part of the house without complaining. I didn't pout. I really wanted a baby doll.

At church, our Sunday school teacher taught us a Bible verse: *"Take delight in the Lord, and he will give you the desires of your heart"* (Ps. 37:4). She told us God would give us the desires of our heart. So, I prayed and believed. I prayed and I really believed. I wanted a beautiful baby doll for Christmas. Surely, Santa would answer my letter, but just in case, if Santa didn't bring what I wanted, God would surely give me the desire of my heart anyway.

A few days before Christmas, a car pulled up in front of our house. Some people put two large boxes and one small box on our porch. As soon as they drove away, Mama and Larry pulled the boxes inside. Mama asked all of us to sit on the floor while she examined the contents of the boxes. The first box had things that made Mama smile very big, but I was not too interested. There were things like a huge turkey, Irish potatoes, light bread, vanilla wafers, peanut butter, bananas, apples, oranges, cans of pumpkin and collard greens, and even bake-and-serve rolls. Another smaller box had nuts, candy necklaces, banana and strawberry kits, bubble gum cigarettes and cigars, taffy, candy canes, and sorghum candy drops. Mama said we would get to pick a piece of candy after all the boxes were opened. We weren't very patient as she first broke the candy cigarettes in half and cut the bubblegum cigars into smaller pieces and threw the boxes away.

When Mama began to take the things from the third box, however, we all became excited. Mama pulled out a softly used baseball and bat, a catcher's mitt, a basketball, a football, a blue jump rope, a stuffed animal, a tea set that had not even been opened, and the most beautiful baby doll in the world. The doll had blonde hair and blue eyes. She was wearing a blue dress with a lace collar that matched her blue hat. She had little white socks and shoes. I was jumping up and down and quietly saying, "Thank you. Thank you." I don't know if I was thanking the people who brought the toys, thanking Mama who held the doll, or thanking God or even Santa for sending the desire of my heart!

Mama held out the basketball to Jerry, the football to Larry, the Teddy Bear to Sue, the tea set to Linda, and then she picked up the most beautiful doll in the world and turned to where I was sitting with my sister Barbara. I could hardly breathe; I was so excited. Mama smiled and gave my doll from Santa and the answer to my prayer, the desire of my heart, to my sister Barbara, not me.

I grabbed the doll from my sister and held it close, crying, "This is my baby doll, not hers." Soon, my mother's voice began to penetrate my thinking. I couldn't believe what she was saying.

"Geneva Jane, give the baby doll to your sister. She has been begging for a doll for such a long time. She even wrote Santa for a doll. Can't you see? It even looks like her. It has blonde hair and blue eyes, just like her. Besides, you don't really want the doll. Give the doll to your sister and take this catcher's mitt."

I handed the doll to Barbara, but I kept crying. I noticed how everyone seemed so happy—everyone but Mama and me, that is. Mama looked so sad. She explained that she was sorry I was so hurt, but she had no idea that I had even wanted a doll. She hesitantly said that there was another doll in the box, and she pulled out the ugliest doll in the world. It had no legs and no hair. Some fingers were missing, and part of its face had peeled. When I looked over at Barbara, I knew she deserved the most beautiful doll in the world because the doll looked just like her. I looked down at the ugliest doll in the world and knew I deserved it because it was ugly, just like me.

I threw the old ugly thing in the back of the bedroom closet and forgot its presence. Barbara's doll sat high on top of the dresser. It was the first thing I saw in the morning and the last thing I saw at night. During the day, her doll sat like a queen in the middle of the bed. Everyone said it was beautiful and looked just like Barbara. But my brother and sisters teased me about my ugly doll that was falling apart. And I knew they meant that the ugliest doll in the world looked just like me. I acted like I didn't care, but inside, I felt unloved, unwanted, unworthy.

A few weeks later, I heard the splattering of the gravel against the side of the house as the car pulled into the driveway. I heard the squeak of the car door and the clumsy, drunken steps of a man coming up the sidewalk. I was already hiding in the closet when I heard the front door slam closed. I heard him shout for the no-good, stupid kid who left the catcher's mitt on the porch. I was as far back in the closet as I could go, but I could still hear the yelling, the slapping, the knocking over of furniture, and as usual, Mama crying and begging. Putting my hands over my ears did not help.

I realized I was sitting on something hard and uncomfortable. I reached under me and jerked out from under me the ugliest doll in the world. I couldn't see it, but I heard it crying and held it close to me. "Shh . . . don't cry, Baby Doll. Don't be afraid. I'm here. He can't find us." And in the back of the closet, God gave me the desire of my heart, not something to sit high on the dresser and on the bed to be admired, but a baby doll that needed to be loved and comforted.

And in the next few weeks, when I would hear the spitting of the gravel against the side of the house, the clumsy, drunken steps of the man going up the sidewalk, and the slamming of the front door, I would run to my hiding place to protect the baby doll. I did not want it to cry when the yelling and screaming began. And each time in the dark of the closet,

God came and put His arms around me, and we both told the baby doll not to cry.

Mama took me to the used clothing store to buy baby clothes and blankets for my baby doll. We stuffed nylons in the arms and legs. Soon, I did not notice its imperfections. Through my eyes, I only saw a beautiful baby doll, a doll who was not stupid or unworthy, a doll who was loved, and a doll just like me.

Thoughts Today

God knew the desire of my heart. While I thought my desire was a beautiful doll to be admired, He knew the true desire of my heart was to feel loved and comforted. No one remembers what happened to the most beautiful doll in the world. But my baby doll—my desire—with all its peeling skin and stuffed arms and legs, has traveled all around the world. My baby doll sits in the corner of my bedroom today, ready to comfort me if I need it. My baby doll reminds me of my safe times growing up. There was so much love in the family despite the need to find a hiding place.

My Prayer of Thanks

Dear Father,
Thank You for knowing what I really needed for each year of my life. Help me to recognize the desires of my heart when You send them to me. Thank You for my baby doll who looks just like me—a child worthy of love. Amen.

A Precious Hiding Place

"In the shelter of your presence you hide them from all human intrigues; you keep them safe in your dwelling from accusing tongues" (Ps. 31:20).

For a long time, my sisters and I discovered the attic as a special hiding place. We could fall soundly asleep on blankets on the middle section that had flooring. The mice running around in the corners did not bother us. We were safe. Other family members soon found our hiding place. Eventually, we would bring more planks to lie on the attic floor joists. Later, soft mattresses and pillows were added to our stash upstairs. And each one learned to pull up the metal chain so the ladder was secure upstairs and we would be safe.

There were several difficulties with hiding in the attic. One was that we couldn't go down to use the bathroom until we were sure Daddy was asleep. Also, we couldn't walk around or talk because the sounds seemed to echo. Sometimes, it was stuffy and hot in the attic, and there were no windows to open. In the winter, it would be cold, so we left the ladder down for the heat to come up. We had to make sure we knew when to pull up the ladder in case Daddy came home early or woke up from his deep sleep.

Mama talked Daddy into having our uncle put big windows at the ends of the attic. He placed a huge fan in one to keep the air circulating. Then, our uncle put a wood floor all over the attic space. We had lots of room to put our mattresses. It was the best hiding place in the world, except Daddy knew we would be sleeping there.

When Daddy was not himself, he would usually forget we were upstairs if we pulled the ladder-door and chain up behind us. He would walk through the house calling our names, but we did not answer. Without anyone to yell at, Daddy would soon fall asleep in his favorite chair.

To keep my sister quiet, I taught Sue to type. I drew twenty-six tiny circles for each letter of the alphabet and another ten for the numbers on a piece of cardboard. She learned to type and spell and even count with her typewriter. Sue would sit on the mattress with a box in front of her and practice typing for hours. She got very good at knowing the letters of the alphabet and the numbers one to ten. Sometimes we would teach her the spelling words from school to type. She became a good speller.

My baby sister didn't want to type; she wanted to teach the dolls and stuffed toys to behave in school. She loved us reading stories to her. She would bring us a magazine or the Revelation book or Sunday school papers so that we would read to her. She didn't know that sometimes we were just making up interesting stories that were not written on the pages.

All of us loved the attic. We could only stand up in the center section, but the attic seemed huge to us. Our small two-bedroom home had doubled in size, making sleeping areas easier for six kids. The awkward niches and low rafters offered places to put open shelves for toys, clothes, and jars of canned vegetables, Mama's cedar chest, and boxes for personal belongings, even the cardboard typewriter.

Sometimes Mama would lie on the mattress and tell us more stories. Sometimes we would chat while Sue typed and my baby sister read to her students nearby on the mattress. We felt safe lying on the floor, looking up at the rafters. We felt special looking out our attic windows, where we could see almost every house on that side of the project.

Thoughts Today

Those loving experiences on the mattress in the attic still make me feel the presence of my mother, even as I relax on my bed. Lying on the many pillows helps me to breathe easier with my oxygen. I find myself using my mattress as a desk as I spread out my calendar, mail, and journals. I find comfort reading, typing, and talking to friends on the phone or checking Facebook while chilling out on my bed.

Sharing the memories of my sweet family lying on the mattress in the attic remind my adult children and grandchildren that they are always welcome to sit on my bed and stay awhile. Now and then, other family members and a few friends come in and automatically sit on the king-size bed just to chat. We are comfortable and spend time sharing about the events of the day, how God is blessing us, and what we plan to do in the future.

My Prayer of Thanks

Dear Father,
Thank You for the sweet memories of our attic, a place where we knitted together as a family. Help me to continue to find ways to keep our siblings together as long as I am able. Help me to teach my children and grandchildren to stay in communication with one another and to realize You are the reason we love one another. Amen.

Coming Up the First Step

"The Lord is my rock, my fortress and my deliverer; my God is my rock, in whom I take refuge, my shield and the horn of my salvation, my stronghold" (Ps. 18:2).

We heard the signs of Daddy being home: the spitting of gravel on the side of the house, the squeaking of the car door, and the stumbling up the steps to the front door.

Time after time, week after week, we knew the routine necessary to hide in the attic.

We knew the drill. Today was no different. We had already run to the kitchen and grabbed a kitchen chair and pulled it into the hallway directly under the attic door. Larry stood on the chair and stretched to catch the chain. He pulled the chain down and jumped off the chair. Down came the door with its squeaky ladder steps. Up we went, one by one, to our hiding place. We quickly pulled up the ladder and then the long metal chain. We wrapped the chain around a nail so it would not fall back through its hole. Then we silently waited for Daddy to quit searching and fall asleep. Once again, we felt safe in our hiding place.

Mama was at work, still plucking chickens. We heard Daddy walk through the house, yelling out names and cursing louder and louder as he stumbled into chairs and tables. As Daddy walked back through the hallway the second time, he stumbled over a kitchen chair. Oh, no! We realized we had forgotten to put the chair back in the kitchen.

Then some demon whispered in Daddy's ear to look up. Daddy looked up and noted that the chain was missing. He climbed on that same kitchen chair and reached his long skinny fingers into the hole on the attic door. The chain we thought was in a safe place was no longer safe. Daddy found the chain and let it fall slowly through the hole. We listened to each echoing clang as the chain fell through the hole. Clang! The chain is falling. Clang! Clang! The chain won't stop falling. Clang! The chain is down.

Grabbing the chain, Daddy kicked the chair out of the way while pulling down the door with its ladder. We sat huddled together, listening as threatening and angry sounds invaded our private, safe room. He had found our hiding place. He was coming! He was coming up the first step. Coming up the second step. Coming up the third step. We already knew the ending of the story.

Finally, Daddy reached the top of the stairs, and his head peeked over the top as he stared at us with his glassy, bloodshot eyes. Our hiding place was no secret anymore. He yelled for his stupid, rotten kids to come down. He backed down the ladder.

Daddy waited at the bottom of the ladder as each of us came down, one by one. And instead of a hug and a kiss, we heard a soft cruel laugh with the words, "Daddy's home." Then it was a quick shove, a well-aimed kick, or a slap as we tried to make it to the door. *Mama, please come home from work.*

THOUGHTS TODAY

Can I say upfront that I did not like my father very much? I did not like the way Daddy disciplined his children. I did not like the way he threatened and abused his wife and children. I did not like it when he smelled of alcohol, chewing tobacco, and cigarettes.

At that point in my life, I probably should have been seeing a therapist, but that wasn't popular in those days. I didn't receive therapy, but I had a daily support group with my brothers and sisters since we were all going through the same experiences. We were able to process our emotions with Mama's help and with the encouragement of Sunday school teachers and leaders who didn't even know how bad our problems were at home.

I can honestly say I loved my daddy only because Mama said I needed to love him. I loved my daddy because God's Word told me to love him. I loved my daddy because God helped me forgive him and then love him. But I never ever really liked him.

My Prayer of Thanks

Dear Father,
Thank You for helping me love my daddy despite who he was while under the influence of alcohol. Thank You for forgiving my daddy and making him Your son again. Help me to continue forgiving him as thoughts of the past come across my mind. Help me to find things to like about him. Amen.

The Good Old Boys

"The Lord is with me; I will not be afraid. What can mere mortals do to me? The Lord is with me; he is my helper. I look in triumph on my enemies. It is better to take refuge in the Lord than to trust in humans. It is better to take refuge in the Lord than to trust in princes" (Ps. 118:6–9).

Daddy was beating Mama once again, but she finally got away and ran outside. He went to the closet and lifted his shotgun off the top shelf. He was trying to shoot Mama as she half-walked and half-ran to the outside so the neighbors wouldn't notice anything. Daddy shot his gun off, missing Mama and hitting the wall inside the house. Then he laughed like it was a game as he walked to the bedroom to sleep it off.

We were in survival mode. We were tiptoeing around Daddy, trying to keep the peace and avoid a blowup. We knew to be quiet, to hide, to run, but now we needed a next step.

We kids talked about it and decided to call the police. It was the only thing to do to protect Mama. The time was right. Daddy was sound asleep on the bed. Mama had returned and was recovering on the bedroom floor half-asleep, half-awake, listening to the radio. We didn't know who was listening on the party line, but we didn't care; we were going to call the police. Both Barbara and I took turns talking to the police. With wide eyes, our brothers and sisters listened to the one-way conversation.

The police hadn't come when Mama first called them, but this time, they came. The police car parked right out in front of the house. The whole neighborhood would soon know the police were there, but we didn't care anymore. We opened the door and offered them seats on the couch. No one sits in Daddy's chair. The two men sat down and listened closely to our stories of fear, of beatings, of Mama's hospital stays and stitches, and big bruises on Mama and sometimes ourselves. They glared at us as we tried to explain our situation.

The police officers respectfully stood up when Daddy walked into the room and apologized, "Sorry, Ralph, the kids called the station and reported a gun being shot, and we are required to come." They walked outside, and Daddy explained to them what happened. The police then told us angrily, "Don't ever call us again. This is a private affair between your mom and dad. It is not your job to tattle on your daddy when he wasn't really trying to hurt anyone."

The policemen shook hands with Daddy as he walked them to their car. They stopped at the car, laughing at something while smoking cigarettes and hitting each other on the back. Mama called them the "good old boys." The neighbors looked out and knew all was well at the Lambert house. They could see the police shaking hands again with Daddy and laughing before they drove off.

When the police car left, Daddy turned quickly from the driveway and walked toward the front door. Daddy was mad. We knew it was time to find a quick hiding place away from Daddy's reach. We all ran out the back door.

Mama waited five years after the second incident with the police. She finally talked to a neighbor about Daddy, and she helped Mama put out a warrant for his arrest for physically abusing his wife and kids and using a butcher knife and firearms. This time, the police officers parked in the driveway behind Daddy's car. They knocked politely on the door and did not try to scare us as they walked in the house. They made Daddy stand up from his favorite chair. He looked at us like we were the meanest kids in the world.

They told Daddy it wasn't the kids' fault they had come. They could get two pieces of evidence, a butcher knife and a gun, if they had to. They also said the hospital had too many records of Mama falling and hitting her head. One policeman was gentle as he apologized and told Daddy to turn around because they had to put cuffs on him. Daddy looked so thin and sickly, with his bones showing through his T-shirt and his shoulder leaning to one side from the many surgeries. He looked so scared as he walked to the car and they helped him get in the back seat. Was my Daddy crying?

A few days later, a close friend of Daddy's drove by the house and shot bullets into the living room, yelling obscenities and for Mama to be good to Daddy.

Daddy didn't stay in jail very long, but it did shake him up, and he promised to quit drinking. He even said he was going to start going to church.

Thoughts Today

Finally, the police did something in answer to our calls. They were receiving training in handling domestic violence from the viewpoint of the victim. Mama just had to wait for society to change.

I asked Mama why she didn't divorce Daddy. Her main reason was that divorce was hard on kids. She explained that we would be talked about in school and at the church. She also said, "I couldn't work and feed you all. Your daddy has his disability check."

My Prayer of Thanks

Dear Father,
Thank You for helping my mother through all the hard times to remain faithful to God and even to her marriage, such as it was. Thank You for helping her give the Lambert family a good reputation as a family with Christian morals and values. Amen.

Pulling in the Ropes

"Our God is a God who saves; from the Sovereign Lord comes escape from death" (Ps. 68:20).

We loved going to Tellico Plains in the summer. It was the hiding place that wasn't a secret. Daddy knew we were there, but he never came to hurt us or even to yell at us. We were really free of danger. We were safe. As soon as we got to the first place where we could see the tips of the mountains, we started singing:

> *Papaw Baker had an old gray mare.*
> *He rode him down to town.*
> *He sold that mare for fifteen cents,*
> *and got the money down.*

Then, as we came to the place where the creek ran through the railroad overpass, Daddy would blow the car horn as loud and as long as he could, and we would yell nonsense as the car drove through the tunnel, splashing water up the sides.

We always waved to the people who sat on their colorful sofa on the front porch of the house near the creek. We felt happy. We were going to Granny's house. We pointed out the houses we recognized, and when we got to Mt. Harmony Independent Baptist Church, we knew we really were almost there. As we spotted the fresh water spring behind Granny's house, we were ready to jump out of the car.

Sometimes we would stay a few days, but as we grew older, we would stay longer and would help with taking care of the garden and canning. Sometimes we stayed at Uncle James's house and helped with the baby.

There were a lot of aunts and uncles at Granny's house. Some of them were married and had children. The boys and the men always ate first at Granny's house. While the women cooked and carried dishes to the table, we girls had to fan away the flies with short branches from the apple tree outside. Granny cooked yummy food and put the cornbread, back bacon, and any other leftovers on the shelf of the wood stove where we could get a snack anytime we wanted. After the girls ate, we carried in wood to keep the fire going in the stove. We carried icy, cold water from the spring and warmed it on the stove as we washed the dishes.

After cleaning the dishes, we felt free to feed chickens and gather their eggs, play on the huge sawdust pile, hide in the corn crib, catch tadpoles, and visit our many cousins living on other parts of the farm along the creek. We would carry water from the spring for cooking, and if we were good, we could go swimming farther down the creek. For safety reasons, we always let my brother Larry jump in first, in case there were any snakes.

As children, we were warned not to climb the huge sawdust pile or dig a tunnel in its side as the sawdust could collapse and suffocate us. We were told not to sit down, for there were sharp splinters. We were reminded that pieces of wood could cut us or put our eye out. They even said there could be a fire starting underneath. None of the warnings worked; it was the first place we headed in the mornings.

At night, Granny closed the windows but left the front and side doors open so we could get some fresh air. These doors leading outside had screens that would let in the cool mountain air but keep out the pesky mosquitoes.

We climbed the circular staircase to the second floor and passed two beds where my aunt and a cousin were sleeping and then past the big salt chest full of pork meat. Dried green beans on long strings and onions braided on a rope hung from the rafters. Jars of canned vegetables were stacked on shelves. Big pots lined the wall in case we couldn't make it to the outhouse.

We kept walking out to the second-floor porch that circled three sides of the log cabin. Uncle Roy was already there in one of the beds. We climbed into another empty bed and slept soundly despite the bedbugs, corn husk mattress, pesky mosquitoes, noisy crickets, cows softly mooing, and Uncle Roy loudly snoring.

Papaw had a room with a door leading to the eating room and another door leading out to the side porch. He also owned a two-room house and store. His cedar cabin was near the wild rose bushes across the Gamble Gap gravel road from Granny's big log cabin. We liked to visit him because he gave us ice cream or light bread with real sandwich meat from the grocery store. He sometimes gave us chocolate candy bars and bottled drinks. He sold most of the stuff to neighbors and friends who stopped by, but we were grandkids and got ours free.

Papaw and Uncle James took us to churches for all night singings that lasted almost to midnight. One time, Papaw said they had snakes in the boxes upfront, but I never saw any. Sometimes, he would ask us to sing. I sang *The Lily of the Valley*, and my sister and I sang *Where Could I Go, but to the Lord*. The men said, "Amen," and the women said, "Bless their hearts." I was fascinated by Papaw and the men spitting tobacco straight across the room into the wood stove in the center of the aisle. They never missed.

I wanted to live in Tellico forever. It was fun, even with all the chores to do. Some of the uncles and cousins drank some homemade beer and whiskey, but no one threatened us or yelled at us. No one seemed drunk like Daddy. I had a feeling of a safe home, and I was happy.

Once, I went with the man across the street to buy groceries for Granny. I sat in the front seat of the truck and laughed at his funny stories all the way. After we bought Granny's groceries, the man bought me a banana. I had never eaten a whole banana by myself before. I thought bananas were just for making banana pudding and could hardly wait to share the banana with my sister.

The man said he was proud of me and introduced me to the men sitting on the porch, rocking and passing the day, telling stories, singing, or just strumming a banjo. He told me to sing a song, and I sang *How Great Thou Art*. They nodded and spat their tobacco past me to the sand below, scaring the dogs that lay nearby. I didn't like the tobacco stopping in their beards.

On the way home, the man stopped on a side road. He talked to me about the banana and its shape. He asked me if it reminded me of anything. He got very angry when I said banana pudding. He told me to rub the banana and think of him. But the man became angry and grabbed my hair, jerking my head back when I kept pleading that I didn't know what he wanted me to say. The man looked like my daddy, and I started crying.

The man drove me back to Granny's house. He wasn't smiling anymore. I didn't understand what I did wrong. I gave the banana to Granny and went to the creek to find tadpoles. I didn't want the banana anymore. I didn't feel safe anymore.

I told my cousin, who told her mother, who told my Granny what happened in the truck. Granny seemed angry as she walked across Gamble Gap gravel road to the man's cabin. I don't know what she said to him, but when Granny returned, she told me to never, ever go to that house again by myself. Then Granny closed all the windows and all the doors. She pulled in the rope handles for the door and tied them to the nail on the wall. No one was welcome to drop by. As we climbed into our bed, I noticed Uncle Roy, who was only four years older than me, had a shotgun nearby. That night, I almost felt safe again.

Thoughts Today

Tellico Plains remained a safe place to spend a few nights in the summer because, like Mama, her mother and our Granny would never let anyone touch her children or grandchildren. It is sad, though, to remember that despite the threat of being molested, we still went in groups to get our special treats for the day. We remained alert, but fear did not stop our desire to have an RC, an ice cream bar, or a piece of stick candy. Perhaps he felt threatened by us when Granny stood on the road, watching us until we came back.

My Prayer of Thanks

Dear Father,
Thank You for giving me great summers with my cousins and Granny in Tellico. Thank You for helping me forgive the man who treated me badly and love the man he could have been. Most of all, thank You for protecting us from the subtle advances that could have become seriously dangerous to us sisters. Amen.

Saying "No" to Daddy

"Children, obey your parents in the Lord, for this is right. "Honor your father and mother"—which is the first commandment with a promise—"so that it may go well with you and that you may enjoy long life on the earth" (Eph. 6:1–3).

At one time or another, each of us siblings took a gamble to say "no" to Daddy. It was difficult because we had it drilled into our heads to "Honor thy mother and father." We knew why. The rest of the verse said if we didn't obey, Daddy would hurt us, maybe even kill us.

One day, my big sister had had enough of the situation at home. We were sitting on the floor, out of Daddy's way, back behind the kitchen table and chairs. She came out from under the table and stood in front of Daddy, yelling for him to stop. With her teeth closed and her lips in a snarl, she told him sharply to get out of the house. When he didn't move, she screamed for him to get out of the house. She pushed him, and he fell over. We all gasped. How did she get enough nerve to stand up against Daddy in such a way? What would he do to her? When would Mama come home?

Daddy just laughed and pulled himself up with the help of a kitchen chair nearby. He slapped and slapped Barbara, but she wouldn't cry. He slapped her so hard she fell to the floor; he kicked her in her stomach and on her back when she tried to roll away. I stayed safe under the table. Why didn't I climb out and help her? The guilt will remain. Barbara finally made it to the back door and made her escape while the rest of us ran to the front door and escaped outside.

Daddy walked calmly to the living room, turned on the television, and sat down in his favorite chair. Soon, he fell asleep. Daddy would only wake up if somebody turned the channel or if the national anthem started playing and the static became louder when all the stations went off the air until the next morning.

We found Barbara holding her knees in her arms, rocking back and forth on the back steps. She didn't say a word. Her face was red, but she was no longer crying. She kept saying, "I hate him." We kids sat beside her, but she wouldn't let us touch her.

I never talked back, and I was never brave enough to stand up to Daddy like Barbara, but I did say "no" to Daddy once. Daddy stopped at the Stop 'n Shop and told me to go inside and charge a pack of cigarettes. I didn't want to do it because I hated the cigarette smoke that made my scarred lungs hurt. Besides, the manager had told Mama that we couldn't have any more credit until our bills were paid. I told Daddy, "No," and hurriedly explained why. Daddy then ordered Larry to go buy the cigarettes. Larry, relieved to get away from Daddy's threat and lecture, jumped happily out of the car.

When Larry left the car, Daddy grabbed my hand and squeezed the fingers until they felt like they were broken. In case anyone was looking at us, Daddy smiled as he angrily said, "You can never say no to me. You are going to get it when we get home." I was not sure what "it" meant, but I knew I did not want any part of it.

Daddy was silent as he drove the car home, stopping at a small gas station on the outskirts of town. He came back with a brown bag. I could tell by its shape that it contained a bottle of whiskey.

When the car stopped in our driveway, I jumped out of the car before Daddy could grab me, and I ran up the hill. Taking the shortcut between the houses and slipping and sliding down the hill on the other side, I finally stopped in the gulley between the two housing projects and walked carefully to the center of the pipe. We often played games and shared candy in this private place. Sitting on the pipe, I didn't know what to do or where else to go. I didn't have a hiding place, so this one would do until the streetlights came on.

Thoughts Today

It seemed when I was a child, most people smoked in front of children, and some teens smoked regularly. Because of secondhand smoke, I now have asthma/crossover COPD.

There was no law preventing me from buying cigarettes for Daddy. Did I do wrong? Should I have obeyed my daddy and just bought the cigarettes as I was asked? Was I really concerned about his health? Was I being prideful because my church said to not buy or sell tobacco products and I wanted to be a good member? I really don't know the answers, but at the time, it seemed important to not obey.

My Prayer of Thanks

Dear Father,
Thank You for providing a temporary hiding place for all my brothers and sisters on the big pipe in the gulley. Thank You for keeping us safe from falling into the dirty water or dry sand below.

Thank You for helping me not to smoke as I grew older. Please help my lungs to improve. Amen.

The Impact of the Church

Who Will Go and Tell?

> *"I will be a Father to you, and you will be my sons and daughters, says the Lord Almighty"* (2 Cor. 6:18).

We met in the pastor's office and used his desk for our work table. The missions' teacher helped us make houses from milk cartons with short straws underneath for poles to hold the houses up out of the water. We picked grass and glued the pieces on the roofs. We then placed our decorated milk cartons on a round mirror, which looked like a village of houses standing in water.

Our missions' teacher told us about the people in the Philippines who needed to know that God so loved the world that He gave His one and only Son Christ Jesus to die for their sins. As we looked at the houses we had made, we imagined children in the Philippines. She gave us cardboard pictures of pigs, dogs, and chickens to place on the dry ground near our houses.

The missions' teacher then asked us eight junior missionary members to sit on the first pew near the piano. After reading some scripture and singing, "I'm in the Lord's Army," she told us once again about people needing Jesus and what the song meant. Our teacher asked, "Who would like to march around the world and tell the world your Father loves them?" All the kids were holding up their arms and excitedly waving them back and forth. All but one, that is. Why would I want to tell the people of the world my father loves them when he didn't even love me? Besides, we were taught to never tell anyone anything about Daddy. While other children were praying and saying "Yes," I was repeating over and over to myself, "I will never go and tell. I will never go and tell."

After the missions' service and the other children went outside to play, my missions' teacher asked me why I didn't want to tell others that God loved them. I said I had no problem talking about God, but she wanted me to tell them about my father. She listened to me as I shared things I had never shared with an adult before. She sat quietly with her head bowed as she listened to me tell of trying to find hiding places. When she looked up, she had tears in her eyes. She then explained to me that my real Father loved me. She said this calling of going to the world is not to share about my earthly daddy but about my heavenly Father. She read another scripture that I didn't know was written just for me:

> "I will be a Father to you, and you will be my sons and daughters, says the Lord Almighty" (2 Cor. 6:18).

I finally understood. I replied, "My real Father loves me. I want to go around the world and tell the world how much my real Father loves them," and then more excitedly, I declared, "I will go and tell."

Thoughts Today

I have often wondered why that pastor's wife did not help us after learning we were being abused. Did she even tell her husband? Do church people still ignore and make a point of not getting involved?

I was six years old when I accepted that call to be a missionary. I did not know that I would need a lot of education and a skill. I did not realize I would need cross-cultural training. I didn't understand anything about financial support. I just knew my heavenly Father loved me and wanted me to go.

My missionary journey has taken me to Guam, Dominican Republic, St. Croix, eSwatini, Trinidad and Tobago, the Philippines, and Papua New Guinea. That shy girl who was afraid to speak up became a preacher and teacher, an academic dean, a president of a Bible college, and a vice president of a seminary. The little girl who told stories to entertain her siblings while they were hiding used those skills in narrative preaching styles to reach the hearts of children as well as adults. I still realize how much my real Father loves me.

My Prayer of Thanks

Dear Father,
Thank You for a church with leaders who cared enough to teach children like me about missions and how to become a missionary. Thank You for calling me to full-time service and helping me fulfill my missionary call.

Help me to be alert to any abuse in my church family and community. Give me courage to become involved enough to discover what is happening and not just sit and wait to see if there really is abuse. Amen.

Our Church Can Be Your Home

"Whoever dwells in the shelter of the Most High will rest in the shadow of the Almighty. I will say of the Lord, 'He is my refuge and my fortress, my God, in whom I trust'" (Ps. 91:1–2).

"Our church is like a hospital," our pastor explained, "a place where the brokenhearted may be healed, and where all the weary find a safe place to rest." The pastor had ended his sermon by pointing to each of us in the congregation, "Do you need to be healed? Do you need a place to rest?" he asked. "Our church can be the place you can run to when you have a problem."

When Daddy came at me another time, I didn't know where I was running. I just knew I had to run. Then I remembered the pastor's sermon. After resting in the gulley, I ran toward the church. It was only 1½ miles to the church, but this time, it was much longer than the normal twenty minutes to walk there because I had to zigzag on the streets, up to Mulberry, down to Ferry, back up to Church, down to Steekee, and finally up to Grove. I ran quickly, zigzagging on the streets in case Daddy was following me.

When I got to the church, I found one of the stained-glass windows on the front porch unlocked. Looking in both directions, I pushed up the window and climbed inside before a car drove by. I didn't need to turn the lights on to know where the nursery, water fountain, and bathrooms were. The streetlights were enough to find my way. This was my church—my hiding place, a place I could run to. My pastor said so.

I went to the nursery and pulled the crib mattresses out on the floor, I stretched out on my new bed and covered up with the baby quilts. When

I woke up, I ate the leftover crackers in the bag near the toy box. I felt at home in my new hiding place.

During the next few days, I told my brothers and sisters all about the new hiding place. They were all excited when I told them about hiding in the church. Sometimes on Sunday and Wednesday nights after church, one of us would feel the need to go to the restroom. We would go downstairs and unlock a window so we could get in the church that week.

To pass the time while we were hiding in our new place, we played church. I liked to preach and made everyone come to the altar to pray. We prayed our prayer Mama had taught us, and sometimes I prayed like the pastor while I put my hands on top of each of their heads.

> *"Now I lay me down to sleep,*
> *I pray the Lord my soul to keep;*
> *If I should die before I wake,*
> *I pray the Lord my soul to take."*

The girls liked singing from the choir loft. Sometimes, someone would play the piano. We loved to take up offerings, and it was certain that we got back every cent we put in. We kept a box of clothes hidden along with Daddy's old army blanket; however, rarely did we need to spend the night. As we got older, we used our time at the church to study, practice playing the piano, prepare our Bible study lessons, do homework, or just have fun.

After several years of hiding in the church at least once or twice a week, a member of the church board asked if we kids could clean the church on Mondays, Thursdays, and Saturdays. He explained that it seemed we were always the first ones to arrive and the last to leave, so we would have time to clean before others arrived for service. Then he gave me a key to the front door of the church. No more sneaking around; no more making up excuses about why we were at the church. I was so excited. I had the key to my first home.

Thoughts Today

We needed no other hiding place now that we had a key to the church. No one but the Lambert children hid in the Loudon Church of the Nazarene. We protected the building like it was our very own home. After I left for college, the younger siblings inherited the key. We proudly say, "We grew up in the church."

Today, all the Lambert children speak of the Loudon church with glowing terms as they remember growing up in the church where they found their final hiding place. And although they now attend elsewhere, my brothers and sisters will always be ready to visit the place they learned to live a Christian life.

My Prayer of Thanks

Dear Father,
Thank You for a church that made us feel a part of a larger family. Thank You for the encouragement and guidance of Sunday school teachers, caravan and youth leaders, church members, and pastors and their families.

Help me to be a mentor to those seeking to be leaders in the church and teach leaders to be alert to those who may be from abusive homes. Amen.

My Church Home Was Not Perfect

"You are my refuge and my shield; I have put my hope in your word. Away from me, you evildoers, that I may keep the commands of my God! Sustain me, my God, according to your promise, and I will live; do not let my hopes be dashed. Uphold me, and I will be delivered; I will always have regard for your decrees" (Ps. 119:114–117).

I loved my church, the pastor, my Sunday school teacher, and the choir members. I loved to hear them stand quickly and testify in what they called popcorn testimonies. Because I was called to be a missionary, I was assigned mission responsibilities, ranging from librarian for the missionary books, prayer leader and chart keeper for Wednesday's prayer and fasting meeting, and vice president in charge of the missionary dramas or stories once a month.

We loved our Sunday school superintendent. He laughed a lot. He organized a caravan group and helped us earn awards. Sometimes, he and his wife would have us to their house. We churned and churned the milk mixture surrounded by ice and salt until we had thick strawberry ice cream. One day, his wife used canned biscuits and taught us how to make doughnuts. They were strong leaders and well respected in the church.

Sometimes, the superintendent's car would be packed with eight or more kids to take home after church. Sometimes, he took his family home first, then the attendees. He would stop at the gas station and buy every church attender a candy bar or something to drink. The best thing of all was that he would sometimes stop at Carl's Drive-in after Wednesday night church and buy us something special. He could afford to do this only when just a few of us came to church. I almost prayed no one would come to church so we would have bigger surprises. But I stopped myself each time.

Over the years, when I attended church and there were only a few young people in the car, the Sunday school superintendent bought me my first corn dog, my first milkshake, my first chocolate sundae, and my first banana split. I will always be grateful for being introduced to such delights.

Our superintendent was also our Sunday school teacher. He helped us get money for camp and drove us to the campground if the pastor or Daddy couldn't take us. He and his wife arranged for us teens to go to zone rallies and church events in the district. They were there praying for us each time we knelt at the altar. He assisted with the baptisms. His wife helped us get material for our home economics projects. They are one of the reasons I am a Christian today.

My church friends represented the family I had always wanted and needed. The connections were centered on love and respect. Week after week, year after year, the bond grew, and I felt my church family encouraging me and supporting me in all my endeavors at school and church. My family extended to the district leaders and camp directors. I felt safe wherever I went. My church really was my home.

I loved being in the choir. One evening after practicing for the Easter cantata, our choir director drove me home from church as usual. He missed the Huffland Drive exit, apologized, and pulled into a short gravel road leading to a wheat field. I thought he was just going to turn around. But instead of turning around, he shut the engine completely off. Unexpectedly, I watched him, as if in slow motion, turn and slide across the seat towards me. I could feel his warm breath on my face. He was too close. I moved back against the door. Putting one hand on the back of my seat and his other hand on my leg above the knee, he asked, "Do you ever dream about boys at night?" He began to slowly caress my neck and lightly rub my leg as he told me about a dream one of the boys in the youth group had told him about me. I was so embarrassed with the story. It made me feel dirty. I wanted him to stop talking. I wanted him to get his hands off of me.

I recognized something awful was happening. I didn't know what to do. I was stuck in the car with a man I no longer knew. I had no place to hide. I had no place to go. And for the first time, I told an intentional lie to an adult. A car passed, blinking its bright lights, and I blurted out, "There goes my daddy's car. He must be looking for me."

The disappointed and scared board member scooted back under the steering wheel and quickly started his car. He drove me the few blocks to my house. He didn't wave or say goodnight but drove recklessly away.

I cried that night, wondering what I had done wrong. Why would such a nice man who didn't drink become bad so suddenly? I sat on the couch beside my mama and apologized for what happened. Mama reached for my feet and began to massage them while assuring me I did nothing wrong. Mama had tears in her eyes but didn't really say anything.

The next day, Mama and I went to visit one of the older women who served on the church board. She listened patiently, then told us to go home and forget what happened. She said the man was a good Christian and a good board member. She told me just saying his name in a slanderous way would hurt me, not him. She said his wife and children would be hurt. She said to leave the man alone and that I had probably done enough damage already. After all, he didn't really do anything to me.

Mama and I walked back home, not saying a word. I was so confused. Something happened, but the woman said he really didn't do anything. So why did I feel embarrassed and hurt? By the time we got home, Mama had made up her mind. She called the pastor on the phone and invited him for fried chicken. Strange that I remember him asking for another piece of "that delicious fried chicken." I had been so nervous; my piece of chicken still lay on my plate. With a nod, I let my piece be given to the pastor.

After the pastor finished eating, Mama sent all the other kids out of the house. I repeated what happened one more time. The pastor did not really believe me and said maybe I misunderstood. After all, the man I was accusing was a faithful member of the church and served on the board. The pastor explained that I had not been physically hurt, so nothing really happened. He asked me to not stir up trouble. My pastor read a scripture to help me through this disturbing incident. "Bearing with one another and, if one has a complaint against another, forgiving each other; as the Lord has forgiven you, so you also must forgive" (Col. 3:13). The Bible, he explained, said that my responsibility was to forgive the board member. The pastor prayed with us. He said we would keep this incident just between us so the board member would not be hurt by false accusations. I promised to forgive. I did not promise to forget.

I didn't know who to trust anymore. Did anyone believe in me? I lost my faith in the church pastor and members. I lost respect for the board member. The church was no longer my safe hiding place. I told no one else in the church.

I felt I had done something wrong, so I didn't warn my sisters. I didn't warn my friends that the board member might do something to them.

THOUGHTS TODAY

I kept quiet as I was told to. Sadly, my church family loosely translated what I said to others as, "Don't believe young girls who accuse good board members of terrible things." The man remained a respected board member in our church. My sisters told me the man continued to get overly familiar with them, also. He liked to give them shoulder rubs and back rubs while they practiced on the piano at the church. He was always trying to get them alone in a room. No social workers were called, child protective services were not notified, and police were not asked to investigate the situation. After all, he was a respected board member.

My friend who attended college with me told me years later that she had been sexually abused by that same man on the way to Trevecca. She didn't tell anyone when she arrived at the university. The respected board member was paying her tuition that semester. I was left feeling pain for her and very guilty, although, I had done nothing wrong. I kept quiet as I was told.

My Prayer of Thanks

Dear Father,
Thank You for giving me such a safe life growing up. Help me to continue to forgive those who wished to do harm to me and forgive those who didn't believe me. Help me to forgive myself for keeping quiet as I was told to do. Amen.

They Know My Mama's Name

"Do not fear, for I have redeemed you; I have summoned you by name; you are mine" (Isa. 43:1b).

My mama did not win a Nobel Prize. Her photo was not on the fronts of magazines. She was never interviewed on television. She was not quoted in books. But my mama was a woman of worth. And in her own way, she was creative and skilled in everything she touched. Mama learned to make patterns and sew our dresses and skirts from flour sacks. When we outgrew the material of the flour sacks, she took us to a used clothing store. Always concerned about having a good reputation, Mama made us promise to never tell anyone we shopped there.

Mama cleaned and cooked for other people. And then she would come home and cook for us. She had all the ingredients and directions to prepare dishes from scratch all in her head. She learned by observation to make southern fried chicken, potato salad, banana pudding, stew, goulash, pies, and cakes. She learned the favorite foods of each of her children and would make them for us when we became adults. Mine was chocolate pie or gizzards while my sister's favorite was fried potatoes.

Mama did without so her children could have more. Mama always said the neck was her favorite piece of chicken. Years later, I learned it was the only piece left after seven people chose their favorite piece.

Mama never allowed us to criticize our dad. She would say, "He is your father, and you must honor him as the Bible says." Mama always said Daddy was sick in two ways. First, Daddy had only one lung, and if the drainage ever stopped, Daddy could die anytime. Second, Mama told us

Daddy was sick because he drank too much alcohol. He could not prevent the man he became because of alcohol. Mama understood that alcoholism was a disease long before the psychologists came up with the vocabulary and definition of AUD (alcohol use disorder).

My mother was a strong Christian woman who prayed for each of us. Because of conditions at home, sometimes church attendance was sporadic, but Mama had dedicated each of us children to God when we were just hours old. She told us that fact often so we would know we were to live a Christian life.

Mama did not always get to church; either she didn't have the car to go to church, Daddy was angry if she went, or perhaps she had bruises or cuts that people could see. Church people didn't always understand why Mama was not a regular church attender. Perhaps no one really cared enough to ask. With six kids at that time, Mama was never invited to a church member's home for a meal or snack after church. No pastor's wife invited her to stop by for a cup of coffee, and no pastor's wife came for a visit.

With little education, Mama was never asked to teach a Sunday school class, serve on a board, hold an office, or take turns reading the Bible. She was never called by her first name but always Ms. Lambert or the mother of the Lambert kids.

One time, Mama had someone dial my telephone number so she could talk to me while I was in Africa. When I answered at two o'clock in the morning, I was afraid something was wrong. Mama assured me that nothing was wrong; she just wanted to tell me the good news. She had a job in the church. Mama was nearly sixty years old when she had her first responsibility in a church. Her job was to shake hands with people in the foyer and then ask them to write down their prayer requests, which she gave to the pastor.

Then Mama proudly announced, "The pastor calls me Delcie. He knows my name!" After hanging up, I cried, knowing that no one had previously made my mama feel needed in the work of building God's kingdom. I wept because no pastor or church member had ever called my sweet mama by her name. I cried because I didn't realize that my mama wanted the church family to say her name.

Whenever I returned home for a visit during missionary deputation, Mama and I would lie on the bed, and she would tell me story after story. It was as if, for the first time, someone had time to listen. I took all she said and hid them in my heart. Sometimes she cried, and sometimes I cried. We held hands in the dark and laughed at some of the silly things I did to hide from Daddy. She would squeeze my hand and kiss my forehead when I told her things about my own marriage that weren't so good. It was as if she was saying, "I understand." She never actually prayed for me, but she would say, "That is something to pray about."

It was difficult being away when Mama was ill with cancer. Even though I had flown ten hours from Trinidad, the nurse said a defiant, "No," as she walked me to the double doors. "Come back in the daytime during visiting hours." But I knew how to hide. When the nurse walked away, I slipped down the hall, weaving in and out between meal carts, medical cabinets and files, cleaning carts and linen bins, past the nurses' station, and into Mama's private room.

I found a blanket in the closet and put on extra clothes from my overnight bag. The room was cool, and the floor was cold and hard as I slipped partially beneath the bed to be near Mama. Exhausted and content, I fell asleep listening to Mama's light snore. I liked this temporary hiding place. I remember when she woke up and found me sleeping on the floor under her bed in the hospital. I remember with great pride when she told the nurses firmly, "Don't you ever dare keep my children away from me again."

Mama survived the cancer and the treatments. But a few years later, Mama could hear birds singing and talking to her. She had terrible headaches. The doctors found a brain tumor, and they would need to operate. This time, perhaps, to spare me expenses in returning home, no one told me Mama was sick and needed surgery. Perhaps no one thought it would be serious. No one told me when Mama went to the hospital. And although I finally understood, it took me a long time to forgive those who kept quiet about my mama's illness.

The doctors said her benign brain tumor was as big as a grapefruit. Perhaps it was caused by being hit on the head so many times by an abusive husband and son. My sisters explained that maybe because of the threat of having cancer again, Mama didn't want to live and just willed her body to accept death. Maybe, but I find it difficult to believe Mama would just give up; she was a fighter, and she still had children who needed her. I needed my mama.

When I arrived at the hospital a second time, a nurse let me see Mama immediately, but Mama was already on life support. I wanted to climb up on the bed and lie beside her, like I always did when I would return home. I wanted to listen to her tell me stories again, but she was not there. I whispered goodbye and told her how much I loved her, but she did not respond.

Holding hands, we seven siblings gathered around the hospital bed that cradled our sweet, loving, and brave mama. We sang "Jesus Loves Me" as the doctors and nurses turned off the life support. The machines grew silent, and the warmth slowly left her body as Mama walked into the arms of Jesus.

> "If I should die before I awake,
> I pray the Lord my soul to take."

Mama was safe—she was home, no need to hide anymore. He called her name.

My Prayer of Thanks

Dear Father,
Thank You for a mother who tried to bring normalcy to our lives. Thank You for knowing her name. Thank You for that pastor who took an interest in all those who attended his church and learned their names.

Help me to be alert to those who may be known as pew warmers but desire to be a participant in Your kingdom. Help me to connect them to leaders and teachers who can train them for responsibilities within the church family. Help me to learn names. Amen.

The Effects of Alcohol Use Disorder (AUD)

My Siblings, the Survivors

All seven of us siblings can be called survivors, even if during parts of our lives, we might have been considered victims. We did not always fit the description of a dysfunctional family, although at times, our family was in chaos. Each of us has been affected in some way by growing up with a father who had an alcohol use disorder.

One sibling in our family does not remember any physical abuse by our father. Perhaps it is taking that person a longer time period than it took me to process the past. Perhaps that person does not want to remember the abuse or does not recognize struggles in the past as abuse. While the rest of us can remember an incident, this sibling cannot recall standing up to Daddy and daring him to "hit or shove one more time." Perhaps the person minimizes what happened and thinks it was no big deal.

Others in the family share similar views as mine as they recall specific incidents. They recall the emotional abuses, including name-calling, withholding love, and threatening physical action. They remember Daddy's intentional use of physical force that included hitting, kicking, slapping, and pushing hard enough for the victim to fall. They mostly remember it happening to our mother.

Although no one speaks of sexual abuse, the girls quietly speak of a father who was becoming sexually-minded toward his children through sexual innuendos in magazines or novels they read and embarrassing them when Daddy spoke of their maturing bodies and their clothing.

Looking back, some siblings remember the subtle behavior over the years by a relative and a religious figure. While thankful that nothing more sexually violent happened in their lives, they realize they were affected by the hidden forms of sexual abuse that can be just as damaging and shaming.

They regretfully recall sexual projections of the adults through their obsessive looks, back rubs, tickling the neck hairs, discussing sexual dreams, inappropriate comments in asking about what happens during dates, and other troubling actions.

We see in ourselves the adult behaviors of those from a home of a parent with alcohol use disorder. One sibling seems to be overprotective and must rescue each of the others. One sibling shows a strong control of emotions and refuses to allow others to be emotional. Another appears more emotional and can't understand why the sister cannot show more emotions. While one sibling doesn't seem to care what others think, another has people-pleasing tendencies. And still, another is so geared toward people-pleasing tendencies that she compromised her own beliefs and needs.

Some of the siblings became addicted to their own vices of tobacco use, alcohol use, or prescription drugs. Some were able to change and control that area of their lives. One became the same type of character as our father with the same behaviors of emotional and physical abuse forced upon others. Another became overly concerned with the lack of pain management and found various doctors to write prescriptions for pain using different pharmacies.

I realize as we grew older, there was less abuse. No doubt because there was a larger and older group of siblings to come together to defend themselves against one person, and this helped prevent some violence. Perhaps being old enough to have a job, visit friends, go on dates, attend church and school events, and knowing the church was open allowed the younger siblings to escape the necessity of looking for hiding places. However, as the older siblings left home, the youngest sibling was left to the vices of the father once again.

When learning our own unique behaviors by a parent with AUD, we siblings each continue to fight our own battles to become the best person we can be. I will share with you my views of the effects of AUD on the oldest and youngest sibling and how I was personally affected by such a parent. Because there are four of us siblings still living, I will not share their story of being a victim or a survivor. Theirs is not my story to tell.

My Prayer of Thanks

Dear Father,
Thank You for giving me brothers and sisters who have supported me through my journey of overcoming physical and emotional abuse. I know they love me and want only the best for me.

Help us each to recognize and understand that our unique behavior and actions may be the result of our specific childhood influenced by not just an AUD father but also a loving mother. Help us to forgive one another when the extremes of our abuse affect us. Amen.

My Sister, the Protector

"Be kind and compassionate to one another, forgiving each other, just as in Christ God forgave you" (Eph. 4:32).

Each of us siblings were affected in some way by having a parent with alcohol use disorder. Barbara, the oldest sibling, seemed to be affected the most. She was sixteen months older than I was. She said she took care of me growing up; she even said she changed my diapers. In a sense, she was right. We took care of each other, but Barbara was the great protector. Barbara often fought with Daddy rather than running and hiding. She seemed to carry the weight of caring for all of us on her shoulders. We did not ask her to take care of us. Mama did not ask her to do it. She just did it.

Perhaps remembering the hurts of her childhood, Barbara often used anger as a defense mechanism. Sometimes, she was not only angry at our father but also at our mother. She blamed Mama for not leaving Daddy, for not getting a divorce, for not doing more to protect us children. Barbara was often angry at her siblings and felt they were plotting against her if we did not do things her way. In her memories, she was the only one who was abused by our father.

Then, in a complete mood swing, Barbara could show great love by buying gifts, clothes, glasses, and other items a person might need. She would clean house, cook special food, babysit, and tutor those needing extra help. She wanted to protect and rescue the homeless on the streets, the hungry in the world, lost animals on the country road, or even a plant needing extra attention. Barbara wanted to help anyone needing assistance, even fostering a child who was overwhelmed in her own abusive environment. She would help anyone in any situation that the person may have, whether a family member or a stranger. While Barbara had a strong desire to "rescue" people she believed needed her help, she may have neglected some of the needs of her own family in the process.

Barbara was very intelligent. She was valedictorian of her high school graduating class. She studied and became a successful hair stylist. With three young children, Barbara went to college and became a successful elementary teacher. The feelings and strengths that Barbara developed to cope with Daddy, she used in her adulthood as she was a mother, student, and teacher. She was hard-working and goal-driven.

Barbara loved church. She was always a top quizzer as a child and as a teen. She sang in the choir and played the piano at our local church and taught Sunday school at another. The students admired her teaching abilities and one time even clapped when she told a Bible story as if the characters lived in today's culture. She loved the music of the church and taught the hymns to her children. She was always looking for a better church that would meet her needs and one where she could feel comfortable as a worshipper. She changed denominations several times from Nazarene, Methodist, Lutheran, to Anglican.

Barbara loved thrillers and the movies that showed monsters and brutal heroes capable of destroying property and killing people. Her bookshelves were filled with copies of thrillers she watched over and over. She was often depressed and in conflict with others. Perhaps having grown up in a world without control, Barbara desperately needed to always be the one in charge. This worked well in the classroom. But she tried to control not only her family but others with whom she came in contact, and it did not work out so well.

If Barbara could not control a person or a situation, at times, she would stretch the truth about a family member and repeat it often enough until even she believed what she had first spoken was the truth. At first, she had the ability to convince others to believe her side of any debate, discussion, or argument. However, some family and friends later lost confidence in her. This hurt her, and she didn't understand what was happening to the family she wanted to protect.

Barbara was truly ill and in great pain most of her adult life. Because of having so much pain, she seemed to some people that she had a substance use disorder. Perhaps for a while, she was addicted to prescription pain medicine and was willing to purchase unused pain pills from her friends to help ease her pain. She had heart problems, kidney failure, and diabetic problems. She had unexplained physical symptoms like stomach pains and severe headaches. Could this have been caused by the kicks on her stomach and head by an abusive father?

Emotional stress followed my big sister throughout her life. I never knew how she would react when I was around. I visited her in Germany and Kansas, and she visited me in Africa and several states in the US. She showed me great love. At times, she loved me and wanted to give me things and do things for me, but it seemed she always expected something in return.

Although I made the highest score on the local examination in high school, Barbara said I was a teacher's pet when I was selected to take the National Science Foundation exam instead of her. However, she was there with me, representing the family when Mama and Daddy didn't come to my awards events. She fixed my hair before I walked out on stage and told me which fork to use at the banquet. She allowed me to wear her formal dress that she sewed in home economics class. Later, she helped me plan my wedding. She took care of me in some way all her life.

While doing so much for me, Barbara resented me for my own successes and tried to turn family and friends against me. She went against my wishes when my pre-teen children spent the night with her, taking them to a movie I did not approve of and allowing them to drink wine during communion. I did not understand her, but I loved her.

In her later years, Barbara regained control of her life. She and her eldest daughter became close friends in a healthy mother-daughter relationship. She tried to become the Christian mother and sister she had always wanted to be to all her children and siblings, but there were many difficulties. She called me once and asked if I could come visit again. Of course, I responded in a positive manner, but before we could visit each other, she died. Perhaps if she had not succumbed to her illnesses, Barbara could have succeeded in being the person she wanted to be. I miss my big sister.

Barbara, my protector. Born January 16, 1945; died February 22, 2015.

My Prayer of Thanks

Dear Father,
Thank You for giving me a big sister who wanted to protect me from harm. Thank You for giving her the gift of storytelling that kept us entertained in what could have been dangerous situations.

    Thank You that Barbara was trying to make amends with her children and reconnect with them before she died. Thank You that she wanted to also reconnect with her siblings.

    Help me to remember to keep open communication with my own children and all my loved ones. Help me to know what effect my parents had on me growing up and learn how to adjust my life to be the best that I can be. Amen.

My Brother, the Seeker

"Nor thieves nor the greedy nor drunkards nor slanderers nor swindlers will inherit the kingdom of God" (1 Cor. 6:10).

Each family member was affected in different ways by an AUD father. My youngest brother Don was born the first year I was in college, making me almost nineteen years his senior. All his siblings grew up and, one by one, left home until Don was alone at home with Mama and Daddy. He was afraid he would always be alone because all his older siblings would surely die first.

Don was always seeking money for drugs. Daddy had a remarkable but sad influence on Don. After Daddy's death, Don was identified with alcohol use disorder, and later, he advanced to drugs. He stole money from Mama to buy drugs. He even took her prescriptions when he found any in her personal belongings. He sold things belonging to family members when he needed funds for his substance use disorder. He continued the ritual of beating Mama just because he could.

The use of alcohol affected Don's ability to maintain any regular job. Unfortunately, he didn't receive a monthly veteran's check like Daddy had always received to take care of bills. Don had his driver's license suspended, hit several parked cars on a street, spent time in jail, and once, under control of drugs, sat naked on his rooftop. He grew up to have many problems like his daddy. We realized that Don was sick and needed help. We tried to help him. We loved him so much.

Don was always seeking financial security but felt his family background ruined his life. When he had to rent or live with friends and owned an old car that broke down often, he accused his brothers and sisters of having an easier life. He refused to listen to us when we explained that going to school many years helped us to find better jobs and make more money. He did not believe that we first lived in smaller, inexpensive houses or rented until we saved enough to upgrade. He didn't believe we grew up with the same daddy, who had the same behavior Don recognized.

We tried to help Don financially. I sent small checks once a month, but some he never cashed. He was always thankful, but later he said it was embarrassing to cash the check at the grocery store or the Dollar Tree because he didn't have a bank account. I paid his electric bill once, and he complained he could have used the money for something more important. His siblings took Don into their own homes when he needed a place to sleep; some transported him to and from work; some paid his court fees; one even bought a small house for him to rent to own. He did not seem grateful for any help. He rarely gave money for the rent and complained that the house wasn't a good place to live.

I don't think Don ever realized how much we really loved him. Don sought our love but never accepted it when our love was offered. In our own way, each of us siblings reached out to help Don escape his loneliness and insecurities and to show our love. But we failed. I was at his house every time I visited my other siblings, but most times, he wouldn't come to the door to say hello. I left food on his doorstep but never received a thank you. A few times, he called me, but his voice was so slurred that I had difficulty understanding the discussion.

Don was always seeking someone to blame. Blaming others for what happened to him rather than taking responsibility was a normal characteristic of Don's character. He blamed his failure in marriage and his lack of a good-paying job on his family background. Don even blamed me for Mama's death. He said if I had gotten there in time to pray, she would have lived. He thought I had a relationship with God that included God answering every prayer request I made. He said if I had really loved Mama, I would have been there.

Don sought life as it was in his youth. At times, Don seemed to remember the good times growing up. He wanted me to come visit and spend the night at his house. He said it would be like the good old days, and we could invite the sisters to play Scrabble with us. For a while, he attended a few family gatherings at Thanksgiving and at Christmas and once at a rented cabin, but the need for alcohol and drugs kept him a prisoner in his home.

Don sought help. There were times Don tried to quit drinking and using drugs, and he felt God speaking to him. He knew he could live a better life. A friend helped him to get into AA (Alcoholic Anonymous) and gave him a way to phone family. We were proud of his progress. But like some users, he fell back into the habit of using alcohol several times.

Don always sought God to rescue him from his demons. Don's young adult years were filled with many fears and struggles with demons of this world, but Don would always reach out to God, even at his lowest depth. He tried reading the Bible and listening to many media preachers and close friends. He could hear demons walking through the house, ready to grab him. He was afraid to be alone. On some days, he only wanted to talk about what heaven would be like. At times, he really seemed to want Jesus in his life.

While some may not understand, I thank God for the timing of Don's death. He was off drugs at the time. He was sober. He was happier than he had been in a long while. He was taking pride in his home and was cleaning up his yard. It was a day of everlasting change for the better. He was communicating with family. Don had been drug-clean for three wonderful days when he accidentally walked across the tracks in front of a moving train.

Today, Don has peace. He is no longer lonely and seeking for connections. He has a friend in Jesus. Don no longer needs to hide from demons. He is with His Redeemer and needs no hiding place.

Don, the seeker. Born February 25, 1965; died October 20, 2020.

My Prayer of Thanks

Dear Father,
Thank You for the joy Don brought into our lives in his younger days and the good memories we have.

Thank You for allowing Don to finally have peace of mind with his thoughts centered on You.

Thank You for opening the gates of heaven on that day of the train accident. Amen.

Myself, the Runner

"I sought the LORD, and he answered me; he delivered me from all my fears" (Ps. 34:4).

I never ran in field day activities at school or competed in a cross-country race or marathon, but I am a runner. As I read my own memoir, I realize I don't face issues very well. I don't say "Stop" enough during conflict. I spent most of my childhood and youth running from my daddy and running to a hiding place.

Escaping to College

High school was over, and I made the hardest decision in my life. It was my first time to make a complete separation from home. I was going alone and carrying the guilt of leaving Mama and my brothers and sisters with Daddy while I went to a college far away where I was safe. I was not brave enough to sleep at home and go to a local college. I wanted to get away. It was what I always did—run. I must find a hiding place, but this time, I will be alone. I left my siblings with Daddy, Papaw, and other potential abusers.

I am older now and still working on myself in the area of letting go of feelings of guilt and failure. I realize that I did nothing wrong; it is just Satan's temptation to make me weaker. I realize I may never forget, but I forgive all the people who may have harmed me in my past. The trouble is that I just need to keep forgiving over and over and over again. I forgive myself for not being able to cope better at a younger age.

I Run from Disagreements

I often feel that my thoughts, feelings, emotions, and behaviors are being rejected, judged, or ignored. When a good friend or family members express their opinions, I get the strong impression they don't want me to disagree, so I shut up to prevent an argument. I run and hide behind silence. The silence allows me to hide my true feelings. When I feel the disapproval of others, I often lack the power to explain myself. At times, I allow people to take advantage of me because I frequently lack the power to stand up for my own rights. I usually just keep silent. But when I do not keep silent, conflict arises.

When I offer simple suggestions, such as offering to assist in cleaning up after eating, out of the corner of my eye, I see my siblings rolling their eyes and making a crooked smile. Do they think I am lazy? Do they think I am incapable of cleaning? I learned to not trust my own emotions as I see these looks. Some friends interrupt me and tell me how I should be thinking. Others stop me if I show emotion about anything. If something greatly moves me to tears, I am corrected and told not to cry. I seem to lose power when I hear those phrases, such as, "Don't be so emotional," "You are too sensitive," "You need to get over it," or "You cry too easily." I lack the power to say, "Stop!" They refuse to listen to me if I want to apologize for something that happened as if my apologies are unimportant. When someone does not validate me, I hear the sounds of Daddy yelling, "Shut up," and I want to run.

I want to run from my family, run from my friends, run from anyone who cannot validate who I am and how I feel. Some statements still cut so deeply; I still want to run to seek a hiding place—my bedroom away from those people who keep hurting me. I know I need to express myself. I need to say to my inner self, "They cannot tell you how to feel." But I run instead of telling them to stop. I am silent, but there are no conflicts.

I Run from Tight Places

I feel like running when I get in tight places. Perhaps at one time, the cedar chest where I hid as a toddler may have given me a taste of claustrophobia that has reached its claws into my adulthood. I don't cry anymore in elevators, but I do go to a corner and stand with one of my children or friends, inconspicuously standing guard in front. If too many people get in, I pleasantly ask to get out. I never go into narrow caves, but I can control myself now to enter a cave with high ceilings and wide paths that might have a train to ride on. It was difficult going into the salt mines in Kansas, but my grandchildren were there, and they kept me from losing control.

In Israel, the guards had to escort me out to get fresh air when we were walking through the Western Wall Tunnels. Tour groups were in front and behind my group. The ones following us caught up with our group and began to lightly touch my back. I had no place to run. I panicked. I like to think, however, that I now have adjusted well to tight places like that as long as no one touches me.

I continually face areas of claustrophobia, such as wearing a mask during the pandemic, being in a crowded room or stadium, and even wearing jewelry or tight clothing. For a few minutes, I feel panicky. I take off the mask and try to be the last one in and the first out when in a crowd. I jerk the necklace and break zippers and pop buttons on my clothing if I can't get the jewelry or clothing off fast enough.

I Run from Darkness

How can I run without light? I always make sure there is some light in the room where I sleep. I once slept in an African home that had no windows and no electricity. When the lamp was extinguished, there was complete darkness. I could not see my hand in front of my face. I had no matches, no flashlight. I couldn't breathe. I began to panic, then I remembered my watch could glow in the dark. Throughout the night, I kept pushing the light on the watch until I eventually fell asleep.

I still want to run away from darkness, even in the US. If the room is too dark, I still push the light on my Apple watch or iPhone and breathe easier. While some want complete darkness—the small lights of the microwave, ice maker, TV remotes, electric chargers, nightlights, coffee maker, computer, and other electrical items surrounding me—all give me security and the assurance that all is well in my home. I am safe.

I confess, I leave the TV on all night, every night. If the room is too quiet, I feel claustrophobic. I must have the sounds to sleep. I must have its light. Perhaps I became used to sleeping with a background of the noises of physical and verbal abuse. Perhaps the memories of sleeping in a room with three talkative sisters and a radio blaring in the background makes me feel comfortable and relaxed. Perhaps hiding in a dark place with no sounds remind me that I am not safe yet.

I Am a Professional

In professional settings, however, I can wear a strong face. I am not afraid to disagree. I can share my opinions. If I am silent, it is because I am being polite, not because I am afraid. I have no need to run. Earlier in my career, I had leaders whose criticism was not constructive and often caused me to doubt my own judgments and abilities. I had leaders who knew about my family background and refused to accept me for who I was and held me to higher, unattainable standards than to others. I spoke to most of those leaders, and their tender hearts were stricken. They apologized for their actions and felt they were just following the lead of my husband. They asked forgiveness.

I recognize now how I got into this situation of running to find hiding places, and I know that God is helping me keep these types of fears far from my everyday thoughts. I have forgiven my daddy and his abusive behavior, the board member who tried to groom me, and the pastor and church members who refused to listen. I have forgiven grandparents, aunts and uncles who didn't intervene, siblings who, because of their backgrounds, sometimes refuse to validate my own thoughts and actions, and police officers who lacked understanding and training in domestic violence.

My Prayer of Thanks

Dear Father,
Help me to control my fear of silence, darkness, and tight places. Help me to stop running from those who do not validate my feelings and who I am. Help me to say "Stop" to those who verbally abuse me. Help them recognize that they are being abusive, perhaps because of their own insecurities in growing up.

I know You have sent the Holy Spirit to accompany me wherever I go, and I no longer feel as threatened as the child looking for a hiding place. I know You will not leave me nor forsake me, but keep reminding me when I forget. Amen.

I Married Someone like My Daddy

> *"But I tell you that everyone will have to give account on the day of judgment for every empty word they have spoken. For by your words you will be acquitted, and by your words you will be condemned"* (Matt. 12:36–37).

I married a theology graduate who was planning to be an educator, minister, and missionary. It was the happiest day of my life. What could go wrong with a Christian husband? His father was a minister who never drank alcohol. However, I explained to my husband from the very beginning that if he ever physically abused me, I would leave him. My husband put his arms around me, assured me that the possibility of that would never happen, and for the first time, I felt safe in an adult relationship.

Is it true that men marry women like their mothers and women marry men like their fathers? My husband was the son of godly parents. He was not a victim of alcohol use disorder. Yet, shortly after we were married, I discovered he had some of the same characteristics as my father.

THIRTY-ONE YEARS OF VERBAL AND EMOTIONAL ABUSE

I had not realized that abuse shows its ugly face in different forms: physical, sexual, verbal, social, and even financial. After only a few months, my husband used words to criticize, ridicule, and manipulate me in such a way as to have a negative impact on my own thinking about myself. My husband called me names for a little incident such as picking up the phone before he was able to enter the room. When I reacted to his comments, he would say that I was overly sensitive or that I didn't have a sense of humor. I did not recognize his comments as being verbally abusive. I believed the things said to me were true. I really needed to be less sensitive. Daddy and my siblings always said so.

My husband seemed to have favorite accusations he used often. "You are so ugly. It is a good thing you married me because no one else would want you for a wife." "If you had a brain, you would take it out and play with it." "The church people laugh at you behind your back; they are kind to you only because I asked them to be that way." "You are a missionary only because they take the wives with the husbands." "You received your master's degree because they felt sorry for you." "If you don't behave, I will send some convincing letters to . . . ." And he would name someone directly in line of leadership above me.

I sought help once with my church leader. "Don't tell anyone about your problems," my leader explained. "The missionary contract is really with the man. You sign only as a wife." I did not tell anyone else for many years. Marriage was important in our church, and divorce was a sin. Besides, if my husband was sent back to the States for poor attitudes and behavior, I would lose my job, my home, and my car. I could not fulfill my call as a missionary. "Besides, it is not physical abuse," the leader said. "It is just name-calling." I agreed; it was not like Daddy, who sometimes beat me, but why did it hurt so much?

Our denomination set up an anonymous call-in counseling hotline for missionaries. It was an excellent idea. I called to see if the counselor could help me be a better wife. The counselor assured me she was there to help me in any way she could. The counselor never asked my name; however, during the second session, she requested the name of the field where I served. She said she had to fill out forms. Since we were the only missionary couple on our field, I knew it would be easy to discover who was asking for help. They would know right away any deep secrets I might share. I didn't dare call again.

When I brought a qualified counselor from South Carolina to the field to work with each college couple individually, I attended our counseling session by myself. My husband said I was the one needing counseling, and he refused to go. The counselor organized a marriage enrichment retreat for the college. My husband refused to come because he needed to work at the church.

After reading a book my son gave me regarding verbal and emotional abuse, I finally stood up firmly against my husband's verbal abuse. I didn't yell or cry. I just said, "When you call me stupid, it makes me feel that way. I have a college degree and a master's degree. I am not stupid. Do not say that again." Of course, he didn't stop, but I was becoming stronger. And I kept saying such statements each time he verbally abused me.

Verbal and Emotional Abuse Leads to Physical Abuse

My saying "No" was the beginning of my husband forcefully shoving me against doorways and walls. He always apologized in a hateful manner. There was a foot often accidentally placed to trip me as I walked by. There was a laugh and a hard punch in the arm when coming near his possessions. He always said he was teasing. He accidentally pushed me down in a gully filled with water from our house drains. My clothes were wet, and my ankle was sprained. He was so apologetic. He pulled a chair out from under me as I tried to sit down. He explained to a student nearby that I often fall. He held hands with me in public, squeezing them until I almost cried out.

Afraid the physical abuse would become worse, I finally told a leader of the physical attacks. He listened and quietly said, "Don't tell anyone what happened. These are minor things that happen in families. You probably are just stressed and thinking it is worse than it is." The trouble is my leader went to my husband and asked him to talk with me and try to keep students from hearing about our arguments. My husband knocked me to the floor, bruising me and giving me a black eye. I told him I was returning to the US. My husband became afraid of what I might say and talked to our leader. My leader came to the house to pray with me about forgiveness and the amount of stress on our lives. The next day as we were driving to church, my husband was yelling words of abuse at me and struck my arm with his fist; I reached for the handle of the car door to jump out of his reach. Someone yelled in the back seat as my husband quickly pulled me in and closed the car door. I don't know what I was thinking. I was not thinking about suicide. I was thinking about escaping and running away. The physical abuse stopped.

The emotional abuse continued. My husband left me waiting outside the hospital when I was discharged while he went swimming. He said he forgot the time. My husband seemed to enjoy locking the car doors and driving to church without letting me in the car. When I did not show up for church, he would tell people I slept in. After I was appointed academic dean, my husband refused to come to faculty meetings or turn in reports. When I was offered an administrative position, my husband would tell the leader I was too ill, too busy, or too stressed to fulfill the requirements of the job. Smiling wickedly, he dropped my academic mail and files in puddles. He did not pass on messages about important meetings. He was out to sabotage my work. I finally resigned as academic dean, but the abuse continued.

I began my hiding games again: visiting students, tutoring, teaching extra classes, and working in the school office after hours. I tried to always have a student to go to church with me so I would have a ride. I tried to get my husband appointed to positions so that he could feel important.

After years of threatening to write letters, he finally showed me written letters full of lies regarding me and addressed to church leaders locally and in the US. He threatened to add a date and mail them if I didn't obey. Obeying meant clean the house, don't have missionaries in to play games, don't have students in to watch a movie, resign your academic position, don't go anywhere, and "keep your big mouth shut."

Divorce, the Worse Sin of the Church

It was at our family Christmas dinner when my husband explained to our adult children that he was not healthy enough to live overseas and would need to pastor in the US. In fact, he surprised me by stating he already had a church to pastor. And while I was mentally thinking how I was going to adapt to this new move, he announced he was going without me. He explained to the family that I was not a good example of a pastor's wife. He was divorcing me.

A leader told us to act like nothing was wrong as we prepared to leave the mission field. During the church farewell, my husband held me close as he told all the mistakes I had made since we were married. Everyone laughed. "Geneva is from the south where they say, 'Be there in a minute' means an hour. That is why she misses so much church when I need to be here on time." "She was so backward," he said, "I had to teach her to wear shoes." He was a good comedian at my expense.

We divided up our thirty-one years of living, and the church agreed to ship our things back to the US. The church gave me three months' severance time. Deputation money stayed on the field. The car stayed on the field. I was no longer a missionary. I had no car, no job, no income, no insurance, and no place to live.

My husband had already emptied the savings and checking accounts. He had already cashed in our stocks. He had a job, a steady income, a car, and a place to live. He said he was a successful pastor because I was not holding him back. I felt he was right. I felt unworthy once again.

The emotional pain was almost more than I could bare as churches canceled their mission services with me. One pastor said that it would not look good for a divorced missionary to share in preaching or teaching in the church. Some leaders said they didn't know what to do with me and then told me to try to go to counseling with my ex-husband, not knowing he was already remarried. Some told me to give up my credentials, even though I did not initiate the divorce. Another leader said, "You should have tried harder, prayed more, and should have become a more supportive wife to a husband who was under so much stress as a missionary."

I had no hiding place except to lie in a darkened room, not sleeping, not eating, and rarely leaving the room. I wanted to punish myself for being a failure. Only one leader called me to give me prayer support; except for family, no one called or sent cards of comfort. No one came to pray with me. It was three months before I could enter a church again. Nashville First Church offered counseling for divorced couples and divorce recovery groups. I went through the divorce recovery group three times, and I began to believe in myself again. The ladies of the Upper Room and the Victory Class helped me heal. A counselor helped me find myself.

Harassment for Twenty Years after the Divorce

But divorce did not stop the verbal and emotional abuse. In between wives (he was married and divorced five times), my ex-husband would write letters and tell leaders he wanted to get back with me, but I wouldn't go to counseling with him. He said he forgave me and wanted to serve on the mission field where I served.

Nine years after the divorce, my ex-husband asked me to go to counseling so I would understand him. He wanted to be a missionary again. He said he forgave me for everything. When I refused to communicate with him, he wrote more slanderous letters to church leaders and friends, and this time, he mailed them. Ten years after the divorce, one leader suggested I resign as a missionary, take my ex-husband back, go to counseling, and be the wife God meant for me to be. Another said, "He wrote some strong accusations. We don't know which ones are false and which are true." Still another said, "Don't worry about the letter; the accusations are too old to consider them at this point." No one said they believed in me. No one said they knew these were all lies. Finally, one leader said, "It is best to not say anything."

Nothing was said, and so the harassment continued. Ten years, twelve years, fourteen years after the divorce, my ex-husband sent another email saying this time that God wanted us to resume our missionary career together. He said he forgave me for all the past problems I had caused. He said, "Surely, you wouldn't fight God's will." Then, "I have written to your field director to talk to you about counseling for the two of us." My ex-husband claimed his wife in the Philippines was not his legal wife since he did not report to the government that he had been married before. He said there was nothing to prevent us from having a successful marriage. When would the harassment end?

The effect of the verbal, emotional, and physical abuse from my father and husband is still there at times, and possibly the verbal and emotional abuse of a few of my leaders.

The guilt still lies deep within my conscience, sometimes hidden, but it remains buried there to be used as temptation when Satan wants me to feel unworthy, unwanted, undesirable, unwelcome, unpleasant, and unacceptable. But I finally forgave my daddy and husband of the verbal and physical abuse. In fact, I continue to forgive them as Satan tempts me by bringing up the past.

My ex-husband called our children a few days before he died and apologized to them for some things he had said and did in his past. He asked them to tell their mother he was sorry for all his past actions and lies. He was sorry for the letters he sent to church leaders. He even recalled a few events during deputation that he was sorry about. It helped that I had already forgiven him many years before and continued to forgive him when some memory was stirred. With a clear conscious, I was able to conduct his memorial service with his Michigan family and our children and grandchildren.

The husband. Married July 17, 1965 – July 16, 1996. Born March 2, 1940; died May 22, 2016.

My Prayer of Thanks

Dear Father,
Thank You for bringing my ex-husband back into a relationship with You before he died. Thank You for allowing him to find peace. Thank You for helping me to continue to forgive him, even now.

Thank You for bringing into my life some leaders who believed in me and many women at First Church who helped me heal.

Thank You for continuing to help me overcome these thoughts of not being good enough. Help me to feel I have some worth. Amen.

Remembering a Loving Childhood

My Mother Loved Me

"Finally, brothers and sisters, whatever is true, whatever is noble, whatever is right, whatever is pure, whatever is lovely, whatever is admirable—if anything is excellent or praiseworthy—think about such things" (Phil. 4:8).

We brought our report cards home and read to our mother each subject's letter grade. She would then tell us to get to the important part of the report, the part that talked about our attitudes and behavior in the classroom. Only after we read the deportment side of the report card would Mama smile and tell us how happy she was with the remarks of the teacher. Her kids were excellent students in citizenship—they listened well, obeyed their teachers, had good manners and sportsmanship, took care of their books, did not talk excessively, and were on time for school. Mama knew what was important in education.

Mama often lay on the floor next to the radio. The volume was soft so no one would be disturbed. Usually, she was listening to preachers or gospel quartet music. Now and then, a country channel could be heard. Mama's love for music inspired all of us to sing and make music in our hearts, whether it was at church, school, in a band, or professionally on the stage. Some made records and continued to sing in church. One directed an orchestra in Music Mansion and managed the music in Dollywood, and others played in bands at local and church events. Music became important as we joined together for family events, weddings, and funerals.

Mama was a strict person about what words we used around her. Despite her father who spit words that stung and abused the hearer and a husband who cursed with words not acceptable by a Christian society, Mama wanted more for her children. Mama reminded us often to never use the word "shut." It sounded similar to a bad word. We were quickly corrected if we said, "Shut the door" or "Shut up." She secretly told us the meanings of words in what she called honky-tonk songs. She approved of the ragtime piano playing but not the words that put down women and family.

Mama did not like it that the Fort Loudoun Dam and Melton Dam were so near our home. We had to be careful in our plans for swimming, park outings, and even church baptisms. She would quickly correct us if the word dam entered the conversation. If I teasingly said that I was going to the church's dam picnic, she would shake her head and just say, "Geneva Jane."

Mama somehow instilled in us that church and becoming a follower of Christ was a necessity, not just a choice. She never insisted for us to go to church; Mama expected us to go, and we would never have hurt our mother. She walked with us to church when she could, even in the winter. After we arrived cold and shivering, Mama would roll up our pant legs and hide them under our skirts because the church did not approve of women wearing men's clothing.

Once we became members of the church, Mama expected us to support church rules and church events. At that time, the church boycotted movies. When a boy asked me to go to the movies with him, I wanted my mama to say no rather than telling a date my church rules wouldn't let me go. "You do what you feel is right," she explained, "You know what the church says." She put the responsibility of deciding on me.

Mama helped us to go to church camp and encouraged us to come up with ideas to make money since she had none. Whether it was babysitting, cleaning houses, or selling the local newspapers, we received her quiet praises. Then, if we needed more, Mama helped us pick and sell blackberries or took another ironing job. Mama was an excellent ironer and ironed not only all the clothes of five children preparing for church camp but our sheets as well. Later, Mama encouraged us to work at children and family camps and others so we would enjoy being away for most of the summer. The younger siblings followed in our footsteps.

Mama said her mother and father never told her verbally that she was loved. She said God taught her to say "I love you" to her children. I am who I am today because I know for sure my mother loved me. Everything she did was always for her children. She taught and disciplined us through words, music, education, church attendance, and by setting an example. She was not hesitant to give me a hug or a kiss. She often said, "I love you."

Mama taught us to dream big and reach for the stars—that nothing was impossible with God.

She would be pleasantly surprised that Jerry, the next to the youngest brother, helped us choose our family theme song when he first played it at our sister Linda's wedding and at Mama's funeral. At every family event now, someone in the family sings, "Somewhere over the Rainbow." The second verse says:

> *And the dreams that you dare to dream*
> *Really do come true.*[1]

Mama. Born February 18, 1928; Died July 25, 1991

My Prayer of Thanks

Dear Father,
Thank You for a mother who never neglected her children, even in the midst of chaos. Thank You for helping Mama to always meet my emotional and physical needs as I grew to adulthood. Help me to be that type of mother, grandmother, and great-grandmother to my own family.

Thank You that Mama gave hugs and kisses that made me feel loved. Thank You that You taught her to say she loved me. Amen.

---

[1] Somewhere over the Rainbow lyrics by E .Y . Harburg, published by Leo Feist, Inc, 1939

My Daddy Loved Me

"Fathers, do not embitter your children, or they will become discouraged" (Col. 3:21).

Daddy did not decide one morning to become an alcoholic. There were some good times with Daddy when he was not drunk. But those times with Daddy when he was not heavy influenced by alcohol were few, yet so meaningful in my memories. In a sense, it is sad to be able to count the times Daddy was a good daddy to me and for me to consider those times his only way of showing love.

Even as a child, I realized that allowing me to kiss him at night was not the same as Daddy giving me hugs and kisses. I can't recall a time he responded with a kiss or hug to my goodnight kiss. Receiving a Christmas card signed "Dad" is awesome but doesn't make up for all the years of not even saying Happy Birthday or sitting at the table when we celebrated our special day. Of course, I have kept every precious letter Daddy wrote me in college or when I lived overseas—all three of them.

Hiding candy Easter eggs in the living room could have become a family tradition, but he just didn't do it every year. Sometimes, he never woke up early enough to hide them. Picking me up at a bus station during school breaks was what a good daddy does, but the times he left me sitting under a streetlight waiting for him after the station was closed ruins my thoughts that he cared. Taking us to Roberson Springs to play in the water or sliding down the Fort Loudon dam hill on cardboard boxes were two things he did that made an impression on me as a child, but sadly, I don't remember him doing anything else that was fun.

Driving was a man's job. Daddy drove us to church camp unless he was drunk. If he was ill, he paid the pastor or a church member to take us. There was something like pride on his face when he drove me to the university to take the National Science Foundation test and the Veterans Aptitude test, but he never said he was proud of me. He never hugged me when I made the second highest score in Tennessee on a science test. I won a summer scholarship with the National Science Foundation to attend college when I was in high school. He told his friends he drove me to the test center. Am I imagining it? Could that be a form of love?

He came to school and church dramas and cantatas unless he didn't. He came to my high school graduation, but not the night I was awarded the title of Future Farmers of America Sweetheart or the time I won the talent contest, and not the night I was given award certificates at the Future Homemakers banquet. He was not there when I won a scholarship. He seemed to see no importance in those type of activities.

Daddy let me adopt a kitten, a squirrel, a rabbit, and baby mice I found under the hedges. He said I could keep them, but they slowly disappeared. He admitted he threw the kitten in the creek.

Perhaps because Daddy was ill most of his life, he was loving and caring when we were hurt or ill. Daddy carried me from the car to Dr. Corrie's office when I stepped on a nail in first grade. Then he bought me a hot dog and a RC when I got home. I stepped on a bumble bee, and my foot became infected. Daddy fixed me his favorite foods: an omelet and oyster soup. It was my first time to ever have such good treatment. Was that love? I wanted to be sick more often.

I think Daddy knew he could win our affections with candy and food. He charged a drink or piece of candy at Carter's for us kids to share. Daddy introduced us to his doctor, who was named Dr. Rock, and his doctor gave us rock candy. A stop at Krystal's and the day-old bakery on the way home from the doctor was so special, but the trip was never repeated with me. Perhaps someone else in the family needed a day with him. Did he plan the day, or did Mama talk him into taking me? I only know I got to go with my daddy.

I felt he loved me when he went to work with me every day at the café near the church. He really couldn't work, but he sat and watched to make sure no harm came to me from the flirting men. At times, he ran the cash register and straightened the grocery part of the café. He was there to take me home every night at 9:00 when the café closed. I was so disappointed when Carter sold the store to Oody's, and their children needed to work in the café. How would I feel my daddy's love now?

As an adult, I had a better relationship with my daddy. He walked me down the aisle at my wedding. He sometimes took Sunday afternoon drives with Mama and me when I returned home for a visit. Mama said he drank less then. The summer before Daddy died, he took me to the cemetery where he wanted to be buried. It was a beautiful spot with a view of the mountains and farmland. He seemed at peace. He laughed without malice and smiled at me.

Daddy became a Christian when he was fifty years old. He became a completely different person, inviting people to church and attending church himself. He no longer abused Mama and Don. Daddy took his grandchildren to the little shop and bought snow cones and allowed them to play at the grammar school playground. Was that love peeping through? Who was this man? That night, before I left to go back overseas, I kissed my daddy good night for the last night. I asked, "Do you love me, Daddy?" As he continued to watch television, he replied, "You know I do." He almost said it.

A week after I arrived back on the field, a missionary received a call and directed it to me. Daddy had died. Another missionary helped me get an airline ticket and leave the country, even though I didn't have the required immigration papers to leave.

Alcohol and tobacco use affected every system of Daddy's body. He died of pneumonia, but the list contained asthma, bronchitis, lung disease, cirrhosis of the liver, weakened heart, and other problems not readily identified.

Daddy never apologized for anything he had said or done in the past. As a father, he never held me or rocked me in his special chair. He never gave me a hug or a pat on the back. He never said he loved me. But in those last few months, I felt he was sorry for the past and that he loved me.

Daddy lived longer than the doctors predicted. He always said that we children prayed for him not to die until he became a Christian; thus, he didn't want to become a Christian because he would die. Not long after Daddy became a Christian, he did die. Daddy is now home with my real Father.

Daddy. Born March 11, 1926; died August 17, 1976.

My Prayer of Thanks

Dear Father,
Thank You for allowing me to have a Christian father for a few months. Thank You for helping me to forgive him again. Help me to continue each day to forgive him.

Help me remember to say "I love you" more often to my family and to people who need to hear those words. Help me to remember that I am loved. Amen.

My Real Father Loves Me

"'And I will be a Father to you, and you will be my sons and daughters,' says the Lord Almighty" (2 Cor. 6:18).

I am not sure how my life would have turned out without my heavenly Father guiding me, protecting me, teaching me, and giving me comfort. I am no longer an outsider; I am a child of God.

I want to go back to that frightened little girl looking for a hiding place. I want to give that scared girl a hug and say, "You are going to be okay. Don't carry any guilt. Nothing is your fault. You are beautiful. You are made in God's image. Don't be afraid of the dark. You are protected. The Comforter is standing beside you."

"Now I lay me down to sleep,
I pray the Lord my soul to keep;
If I should die before I wake,
I pray the Lord my soul to take."

I want to say to that confused teenager. "Dream big. The dreams are God-given. Believe in yourself—the way God made you. You are called. You will succeed in that call based on your Father's love."

And the dreams that you dare to dream
Really do come true.[2]

---

[2] (Somewhere over the Rainbow lyrics by E.Y. Harburg, published by Leo Feist, Inc, 1939)

I want to say to that timid adult, "Stand strong against verbal abuse given by weak people. You are not who they say you are. Your words, your writing, and your thoughts are worthy to be heard because they are a reflection of God in your life. You do not need to keep silent. Your real Father loves you."

> "See what great love the Father has lavished on us, that we should be called children of God! And that is what we are!" (1 John 3:1a).

If You Need Help

If you or someone you know is in danger or is having a medical emergency—call 911 and go or direct them to your nearest emergency room.

If you or someone you know is facing sexual abuse—call the National Sexual Assault Hotline at 800-656-HOPE (4673).

If a parent is hurting you—call 800-4-A-CHILD (1-800-422-4453) to talk to someone.

If anyone is concerned about their own or a loved one's drinking habits and behavior—call or contact the following organizations for information, confidential help, and referrals:

- Alcohol and Drug Helpline: 800-527-5344
- National Council on Alcoholism and Drug Dependence, Inc.: 800-622-2255
- SAMHSA: 800-662-4357

If you or someone you know is struggling with alcohol use disorder, and you want to speak with a trained crisis counselor:

- Text 988
- iChat <u>988-lifetime.org</u>
- Text your zip code to 435748

If you feel you or someone you know desires to seek spiritual help—call your pastor or a pastor from a local church you respect.

Printed in the USA
CPSIA information can be obtained
at www.ICGtesting.com
LVHW071053290224
772930LV00018B/1075